H. BARNES-MOSS
JULY 1981

Living in Spain Today

By the same author

Why Not Live in Spain?
Discovering Spanish Wine

LIVING IN SPAIN TODAY

John Reay-Smith

London

Robert Hale Ltd

First published in Great Britain 1980
Reprinted 1981

ISBN 0 7091 8119 1

Robert Hale Limited
Clerkenwell House
Clerkenwell Green
London EC1R 0HT

Photoset, printed and bound
in Great Britain by
REDWOOD BURN LIMITED
Trowbridge & Esher

Contents

Author's Note

The information as to British and Spanish laws at the present time is given to illustrate their effect on British residents and tourists and cannot be used to support any claim.

Illustrations

Photographs by courtesy of the Spanish Ministry of Commerce and Tourism, with the exception of the last two which are by courtesy of Bodegas Torres and González Byass respectively.

MAPS

Acknowledgements

The aim of this book is, as far as possible, to answer all the questions that arise when a British Subject is thinking of living in Spain, and particular care has been taken to ensure that the legal and financial information is accurate and up to date.

I have therefore sought, and received, considerable help from official sources in both Britain and Spain, and I wish to record my thanks for the time and trouble taken by many busy men in supplying invaluable information and explaining technical matters.

I am also grateful to Bufete Dexeus, Associated Lawyers of Barcelona, for answering questions on a number of matters, particularly the recent Spanish Wealth Tax and the present rates of import duties and taxes on cars.

Finally, my thanks are due to the Spanish Ministry of Commerce and Tourism who supplied photographs used for illustrations and gave permission for their reproduction.

JOHN REAY-SMITH
November 1979

To Marcelle

CHAPTER 1

The Dream that came True

"It has been nice knowing you – I hope that you are doing the right thing."

I remember so well those words. They were spoken to me by an old friend, a chartered accountant, nearly ten years ago.

I had just announced that I had decided to give up practising as a solicitor in the north of England and start a new life in southern Spain. The decision surprised everyone, for I was still many years away from the normal age of retirement – but I thought I saw a glint of envy in several eyes.

Why did I do it? My wife thinks that she persuaded me. She had the idea that I was working too hard and that the sunny climate of Spain would be good for my health. I think that it was originally my idea. But whoever thought of it first, neither of us has ever had regrets. I suppose the truth is that we both did it for the same reason. We did it for fun – and in search of new qualities in life. Our children had grown up, and we were free to make a choice, so we chose a life in Spain.

Other friends expressed their doubts. Would we spend all our time sun-bathing and drinking? Well, of course, we often sit in the sun, and we do enjoy a drink, particularly Spanish wine, which has improved so much these last few years, but Spain holds more than that.

I had realized how important it was to have something to occupy one's mind, otherwise, after the "honeymoon period", boredom can set in, and nobody wants that. So I decided to write a book about retiring to Spain. I had gone through the experience of emigration and felt that I could help others who were thinking along the same lines. Then I wrote another book and articles about Spain and translations of Spanish books.

In that first book I said that "inside every tired busy man there is a little man dreaming of the sun." I still believe that. My "little man" is busy now, but not tired – and the dream has come true.

In the musical play *South Pacific* there was a song called "Happy Talk" with the words, "If you don't have a dream, how you gonna have a dream come true?" So I suggest that you do a little dreaming about life in Spain. The object of this book is to help that dream come true.

It is about living in Spain, and not only for those who make a permanent home there but also for those who make their annual pilgrimage to the sun or decide to work in Spain. I have tried, so far as is possible in a single book, to answer all those questions that are bound to arise when one decides to live in another country. I hope it will enable you to make the right decisions and solve some problems.

Several chapters deal with legal matters and explain various British and Spanish laws that will affect British emigrants to Spain, but they are not a substitute for professional advice from a British and a Spanish lawyer. Laws can change, and frequently do, and no two persons' circumstances are exactly the same. All I can do is to explain some mysteries, clear up popular misconceptions and make suggestions.

Spain today offers a very pleasant and sociable life, but it is important to have something to do between parties and lying in the sun. It may be some absorbing hobby, or a job which satisfies the natural creative desires and at the same time generates some extra pesetas to cope with rising costs.

Among our British friends there is a young couple who run a very popular restaurant and another who cater, most successfully, at local parties. I know a man who teaches English and another who restores valuable paintings. A young widow takes an active interest in the affairs of her local community as treasurer to the Association of Owners, and there is a Scotsman who manages a nursery garden. A retired quantity surveyor and his wife have a general store, and we know a retired detective whose whole life is centred round a basset hound that has won several prizes at shows all over Spain. He had previously trained police dogs. There is no end to the occupations of British expatriates in Spain today, and in a later chapter I deal with this in more detail.

I was recently asked if my life here in Spain had turned out exactly as I had imagined, and I had to admit that it had not. And how dull it would be if everything was just as planned. In these last few years there have been changes in Spain – some have brought problems while others have been unexpected blessings.

A few years ago nobody could have anticipated that prices could rise by twenty-five per cent and more a year in Britain, and Spain too has suffered from inflation. The floating of the Pound in the summer of 1972 came as a surprise, and instead of 168 pesetas, it is now worth around 143. These two factors have increased the cost of living in Spain for British residents, particularly if their whole income is derived from Britain. No longer is Spain a very cheap country, but, as I explain later, it is still possible to enjoy a given standard of living on a much lower gross income than would be possible at home.

When we first came to Spain, I thought that it would be just possible for a couple to live a simple but comfortable life on their British State pension, but today they would need considerably more, perhaps twice as much. However, recently the position of British pensioners has improved. Originally the British pension was frozen at the rate prevailing at the date of emigration, and over the years this caused great hardship to those who had little other income. Spain now has a Reciprocal Agreement with Britain, so that British pensioners are entitled to receive all increases in their pensions, just as if they were still living in Britain.

Another Reciprocal Agreement allows pensioners, and this includes widows under sixty, to join the Spanish National Health Service on payment of a monthly contribution. In most Spanish towns today there are modern, well-equipped hospitals available on the National Health.

Until October 1979 the amount of Sterling capital one could take to Spain without paying the Investment Currency Premium was limited, and the Premium was payable on some property purchases. Today the Premium has gone and there is no limit to the money that can be taken to Spain. This makes emigration much simpler and even more attractive.

What other pleasant surprises have there been since I came to Spain? It is a beautiful country with a wonderful climate, but that I already knew as a tourist. There have been many unexpected things which are appreciated only when you live here.

I had not realized before quite how nice the Spanish people are and the warm welcome they are prepared to offer to foreigners in their midst. We live in a small village beside the Mediterranean and soon felt at home. The tobacconist in the local *estanco*, the village postman and the owner of the supermarket all give one a smile and are ready for a chat. Some try out their English on you, and you practise your Spanish on them. When we first arrived, there was a water-carrier with his donkey. Soon I got to know the donkey by name, and then I felt that I really did belong.

As our Spanish improved, we made friends with the Spaniards living in the adjoining flats. It is very important when you live here to speak the language, at least well enough to communicate. On holidays as a tourist you can get by with a few words from a phrase-book, but as a resident you must meet and talk to Spaniards – and do not worry about the exact word or the correct tense or the proper pronunciation, it will all come in time. There are some British residents, and people of other nationalities, who never make the effort to speak Spanish. As someone so aptly said, "They live like Trappist monks, unable to communicate."

This is a great pity because they miss so much of the enjoyment of Spain, and one is tempted to ask why they chose to live here if they are not prepared to make the effort to learn the language. Some pick it up very quickly, while for others it takes time. But do not worry and do not be shy – just keep on talking.

One of the first things I discovered about the Spaniards was that they are naturally cheerful and gay and have a great sense of humour. They are individualists, full of personality, and enjoy family life. Many of them spoil their children and spend large sums on their clothes and toys. It always amazes me how these children, so often noisy and destructive and rarely corrected or punished, grow up to be such nice people.

Only a few years ago there was real poverty in many parts of Spain. In our village some children were poorly dressed, and their parents lived in shacks on the beach which were made out of drift-wood and beaten-out oil-drums. But today all that has changed. The children wear shop-bought clothes and ride around on gleaming new bicycles, while their parents live in the modern blocks of flats that are springing up everywhere.

Poverty still exists in Spain, but great improvements have been made these last five years. I remember when parts of the main road from Cádiz to Málaga were narrow tree-lined lanes with hardly room for vehicles to pass. Now they are broad highways with wide verges. A town as large and as important as Algeciras had no traffic-lights. Today it has so many that they can be quite confusing.

When we first came to live here, there were few good shops, and in the country a telephone was a rarity. To telephone England one had to book a call with the local operator and wait for hours. Today there is an automatic service over most of the country, and one gets through in a few seconds. In our local town there are now many shops where it is possible to buy everything from colour television sets and tape-recorders to well-made clothes and sports gear.

For centuries Spain has been a mysterious, little-known country hiding behind the Pyrenees – a legendary place of castles, bull-fights, guitars and *flamenco*. It was a beautiful but rather savage country lost in the Middle Ages and dreaming of past glories. It is difficult to believe that only in the second half of this century it has become a mecca for tourists, and even more recently a wonderful place to live in.

But it is not only in material matters that such rapid progress has been made. Just over three years ago General Franco died, and forty years of rigid military dictatorship came to an end, but already the Spanish people have overwhelmingly voted for a new democratic constitution. When I first read the *Constitución Española*, I was amazed what a modern and civilized democracy Spain had become. Many other European countries could learn from it. It will affect everyone who lives in Spain, whatever their nationality. In an appendix I have set out a summary of those provisions that will apply to British residents. This modern democracy was something I had not expected when I first came to live in Spain.

You may think that I am prejudiced about Spain, and of course you will be right. But who could live eight years here without being prejudiced? The glorious sun, the vivid colours, the excitement, the laughter and the friendliness of the Spanish people are bound to get you in the end.

I am no longer dreaming. My dreams have become realities.

CHAPTER 2

Where to Live

This is the first and most important decision, and be made in a hurry. A secondary consideration is rent or buy a property.

For the permanent resident in Spain buying preferable because property is an investment th certainly bound to increase in value. Today both flats can double their value in only a few years. also means that a property can be altered and one's own particular needs without having first landlord's permission, or making a present to increase in value. An owned property more easil true home.

If possible, buy sometime before you emigra live in another country involves a lot of prepar there is already a house or flat just waiting for in, it makes everything so much easier. It is a take a holiday in the part of Spain you fancy good look round before you commit yourself.

Alternatively, arrange to rent a property for months after emigration, and take plenty of tim final decision. The ideal place in July and Augu very different in December and January. Man already have fallen in love with a particular Sp which they return year after year: the miles of and the gay night life are just what they need fo holiday in the high summer, but what is it like

the year when the other tourists have left, the shore is deserted and your favourite night spot closed? A holiday is like a brief flirtation with a pretty girl – very pleasant, but do you really want to live with her year after year?

Spain is a large country, second only to France in size, and in addition there are the beautiful Spanish islands. It offers a tremendous variety of climate and scenery. Whatever your particular requirements may be, you are almost certain to find them in Spain.

First, there is the north-west of the country, the Atlantic coast with its hundreds of little fishing ports and picturesque villages. Here Spain is a green country with a climate that has been described as a warmer version of southern Ireland, Cornwall or Brittany but more mountainous; a region where there is rain and mist as well as sunshine, where primroses and violets bloom beside magnolias and camellias, and where one may even hear the skirl of bagpipes up in the hills or see a Spaniard wearing the kilt. It is not at all typical of the est of Spain and is far from the roar of the gold-rush tourist levelopments. This is the only region which was never conquered by the Moors, and many Spanish aristocratic amilies, who first won fame in the struggle against the nfidel, have their roots deep in the soil. A country of great eauty, with its elegant cities such as Santiago de Compotela, Santander and San Sebastian, it has many devotees for vhom the rest of spain has little appeal. But it is not for the un-worshipper, for it rains on average one day out of three, nd even more on the northern coast near the French froner.

Let us move on to Mediterranean Spain, so much better nown by the British, and first to the Costa Brava and Costa orada. This is the Spain I first knew long before the tourist oom of the sixties. Then it was a place of rugged beauty ith miles of twisting road along the coast and pine trees owing right down to the sea. Round every corner there ere vistas of little fishing villages and deserted beaches. oday one has to accept the high-rise blocks of holiday flats

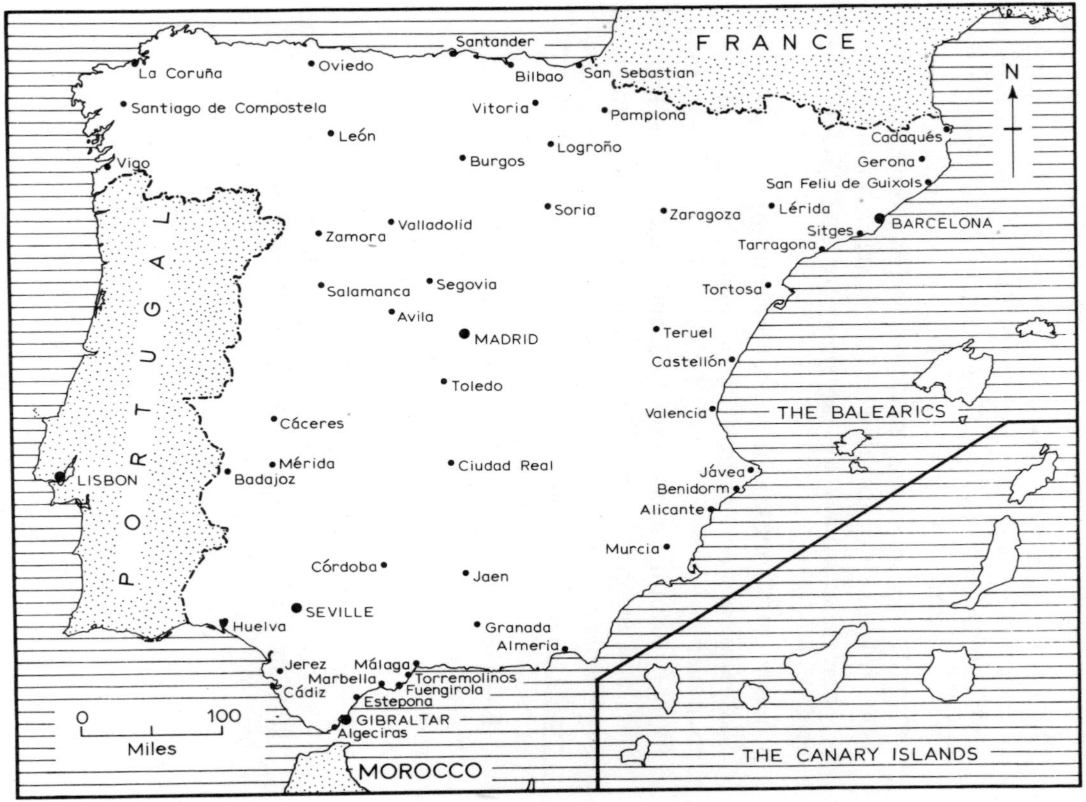

The Spanish Mainland

and tourist hotels, the night-clubs and the razzamatazz of the holiday invasion from northern Europe. There are, however, still places to be found which maintain their charm and character. Las Rosas, Cadaqués – renowned for its painters and writers – and Palamos could be ideal places in which to live. Further south there is Sitges, which, although a popular holiday resort, is an attractive place, and also the charming fishing village of Cambrils. If you prefer a town, then San Feliu de Quixols or its suburb S'Agaro may be the answer.

These Costas have the advantage of easy access, being close to Barcelona airport and only two days' drive from the Channel ports, but for the permanent resident there are other factors to consider. There are more extremes of climate here than further south. In July and August it is hot – often 90°F or more – but the winters are cold, and snow is found inland. Bars and restaurants have become accustomed to charging tourist prices, and property prices in the most sought-after places are high. On the other hand, there is a plentiful supply of beautiful Catalan wine.

Next we come to the Costa Blanca with its main cities of Valencia and Alicante – again a popular tourist area, particularly in the northern part, but, with the exception of Benidorm, not as highly developed as the Costa Brava and the Costa del Sol. Its climate is better. In August the average temperature is just over 90°F in the day and just under 70°F at night. In winter it reaches about 60°F by day and falls to around 45°F at night.

This coast is one of the driest in Spain, where the rainfall averages only 20 inches a year, mostly in the spring and winter. On the whole, property prices are lower here than in the northern and southern Costas. Jávea and Altea are the districts most popular with foreign residents, who number respectively six thousand and two thousand at the present time. One third of Jávea's residents are British, and it has the distinction of being described by the World Health Organization as having an environment that is "almost as perfect as it is possible to obtain". Here one can live in relative peace, as the small beaches and absence of too many large hotels keep away the "package tours".

Taking the long-term view, a little further south from Alicante, round the south-east corner as far as Almeria, is well worth considering. Today it is little developed because of lack of communications, but the new international airport at Almeria and the proposed new coastal road from Málaga will in time change all that, and property and land values are therefore bound to escalate.

Another undeveloped Coast on the other side of Spain is the Costa de la Luz – the Coast of Light – which runs from Huelva near the Portuguese border for nearly two hundred miles to Tarifa, which has the distinction of being the most southerly town in Europe. It is an attractive part of Spain, with miles of golden sand and little white villages gleaming in the sun. Roads and services are good, with an international airport at Seville and a national one at Jerez de la Frontera. A motorway connects Seville with Cádiz. At Sanlúcar de Barremeda is the Coto Doñana park, Europe's largest wildlife preserve.

The purchase of a property on this coast would almost certainly turn out to be a good investment, and, away from Cádiz, prices are very much lower than in Britain or on the other Spanish Costas. The only disadvantage of living here is that it lies on the Atlantic coast and so is at times very windy. Shopping facilities are also few and far between, except in the centre round the sherry area, between Sanlúcar de Barremeda and Chiclana.

I have always thought how pleasant it would be to live in Seville, that most elegant of cities, or in Jerez de la Frontera, which has a personality all its own. Here one could enjoy a comfortable, civilized life within easy reach of the sea, but in either town the cost of living would certainly be high.

The remaining coastal area of mainland Spain lies from Nerja on the east to Algeciras on the west, and contains the most famous Costa, the Costa del Sol, with eighty miles of golden beaches from Málaga to Estepona. Every year more and more British people choose this as their home in the sun, and it certainly has every facility for a full life, with its many internationally famous golf courses and yachting harbours, its fishing, polo and glittering night life.

The climate is temperate, being less hot in summer and warmer in winter than on the eastern coast, and usually there are only a few rainy days in winter. Land values have rocketed on the Costa del Sol in the last fifteen years. Land near the beaches used to cost only 30 pesetas a square metre, but today 3,000 pesetas is normal. Many little fishing villages have become bustling tourist centres – Torremolinos is the outstanding example, and Marbella is now the centre of the international jet-set. Not the best place in which to live permanently, you may think, yet between the tourist centres there are still some pleasant, unspoilt bays, and inland many good-quality developments exist, where, at a price, one can find peace and privacy. To the west of Estepona this coast is much less developed, and prices are lower, with the exception of Sotogrande, where a number of Americans and Spaniards live. When the frontier opens between La Linea and Gibraltar, property values will appreciate rapidly.

The Bay of Algeciras is now a large industrial area with an oil-refinery, a power-station, a steel-mill and many other factories. This will never become a tourist area, and some British residents feel that this is an advantage. Many live in the surrounding villages, or in flats opposite the harbour in Algeciras. Here one is living in the real Spain and not in the often artificial atmosphere of modern developments built only for foreigners. A few minutes drive by car and you are in the unspoilt countryside.

Finally there are the Spanish islands, starting with the Balearics, world-renowned for their beauty. Places worth consideration are Formentor on Mallorca, Portinax on Ibiza and Cala Galdana on Menorca. The bad image of these islands as holiday areas for cheap package-tours is mostly undeserved and should not deter future British residents, as ninety per cent of the area is not affected. Prices of land show great variations from 50 pesetas a square metre for inland rural areas to as much as 10,000 on the coast, and even 50,000 on the front at Palma.

Many have chosen the Balearics for retirement. It is estimated that Mallorca, which is about the size of Cornwall, has well over ten thousand British residents. There are good communications by sea and air; medical facilities are excellent, and in Palma the shops are well stocked.

Which of these islands is the best choice? Each of the three has its individual characteristics. The best answer I can give is to use the words of one long-term resident – "Mallorca is brash, commercial, busy and middle class: Ibiza trendy, hippy and artistic: Menorca aristocratic and aloof." This range should be able to satisfy all island-lovers.

Those whose dreams are to travel further afield and really to "get away from it all", should think about the Canary Islands. Although they have been Spanish for close on five hundred years, they are more African than European, and indeed the most easterly islands lie within seventy miles of the African coast.

The climate in most parts is almost endless English summer, varying from 15° to 20°C (59° to 68°F), but the humidity is high. However, on the highest mountains there is perpetual snow. Of the seven islands only four, Gran Canaria, Tenerife, Fuerteventura and Lanzarote, are suitable for permanent residence. On the others the public services, medical facilities and communications are no more than the bare minimum.

The best places to live are considered to be the south of Gran Canaria, with its continuous sun, and the Orotava valley on Tenerife where it is cooler, and there is a less arid climate and a greener landscape.

The Canaries are different from Spain, and even their laws are different. There are no import duties, and the maximum size of a building site that can be owned by a foreigner is 3,000 square metres, as against 5,000 on the mainland. In addition, as also in the case of the Balearics, Government

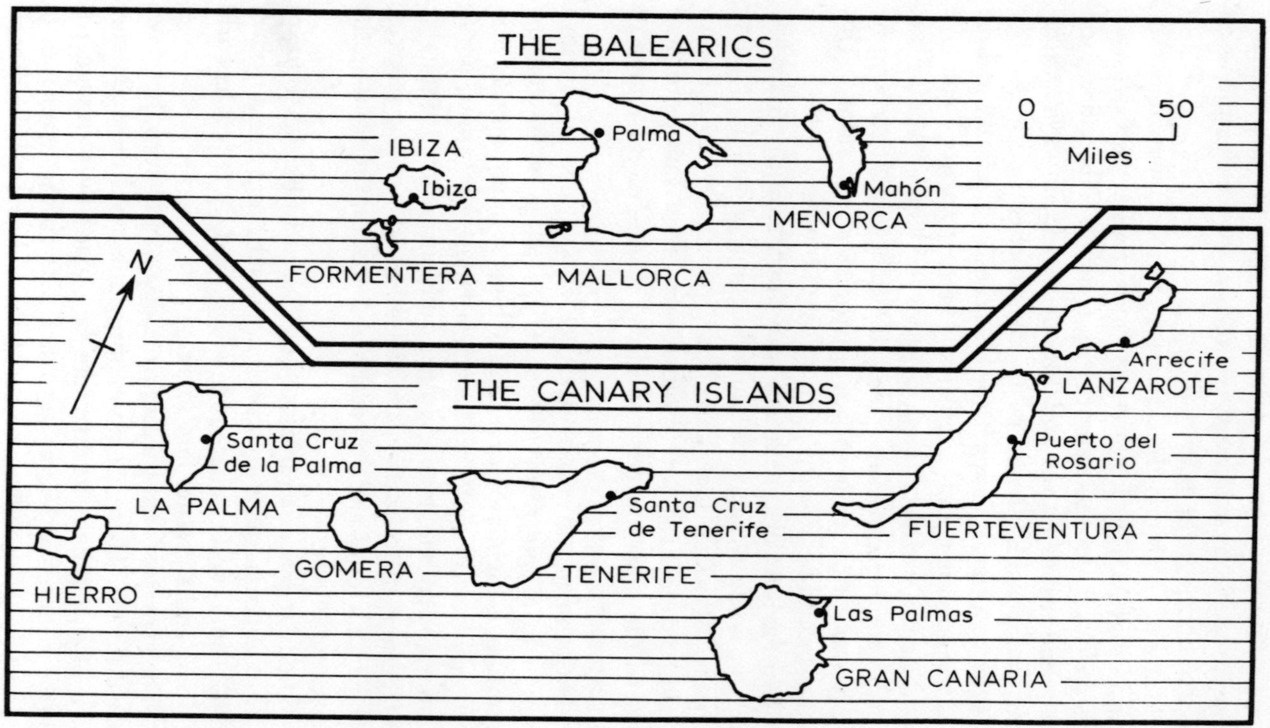

The Spanish Islands

permission is required to own any property, though this is seldom refused. Compared with British prices, property is cheap. Prices vary considerably, but a small flat in a block can be had today for £5,000, a villa of 150 square metres for £14,000 and a luxury house twice that size for about £36,000. The cost of living is very much the same as on the mainland. Some local products are cheaper, but anything that has to be imported is much more expensive.

Now we come to the question not only of "where to live" but "what to live in". Choosing a home is a very personal thing and a very important one, second only to choosing a husband or wife. But if you do make a mistake over a property, it is perhaps a little easier to correct.

Your choice in Spain will probably be quite different from what you wanted in England. Before I came to Spain, I had nearly always lived in the country, and in what today would be considered large family houses with gardens of about three-quarters of an acre. At one time my garden extended to two acres, and the constant battle against nature gave me plenty of physical exercise at weekends. On the whole I won that battle – but only just. When you are bringing up a family, you need plenty of room, both inside and out. Today the two of us live in a flat of 100 square metres with a living-room, a small balcony, two good-sized bedrooms and two bathrooms. We find it is just what we want. My gardening activities are now limited to mowing my children's lawns when on holiday in England.

One's choice is, of course, largely dependent on financial considerations. If you can afford it, a house has the advantages of plenty of room and privacy, and the pleasure of your own garden and private swimming-pool. In the right locations domestic help is available, and a full- or part-time gardener. There is, however, the danger of finding yourself isolated and too far from the real Spain. A few years ago I saw a development up the coast of fairly new large houses far from the nearest town and with a restaurant as the only amenity. There was a surprising number of re-sale notices.

Apparently two or three years there had been enough for most owners. A nearby golf-course or community centre would have given some of them an inducement to stay in what were really attractive, well-built houses.

For lower income groups smaller houses grouped together in a village community on the outskirts of a large town have many advantages. There are several such "*pueblo*" developments along the Spanish Costas. They are close to shops, and there are neighbours to join in club activities. Also they need little or no help to run. From an investment point of view, a beach-side property is nearly always a good buy, especially if you can get into a well-planned development in its early stages.

For many, a modern flat will be the answer, provided that the community is well-run and there is an efficient staff to deal with repairs. You will often have the advantage of a communal well-laid-out garden and a swimming-pool. Today flats are much better built than they were some ten years ago. The aspect is important, not only when considering the view and whether one day it may be obstructed, but also whether it is sheltered from prevailing winds and direct sun. One flat I know is like a furnace in summer and an ice-box in winter.

Which floor a flat is on can make a big difference. The higher it is, the more privacy you will have. If the block is near a busy thoroughfare, it is necessary to be on the fifth or sixth floor to escape the traffic roar. On the other hand a flat or a penthouse on the top of a high block can be too hot in summer and cold and windy in winter. The best is often in the centre of a block, where it is protected on all sides. It is surprising how seldom noise is heard from the neighbours. Noise usually travels upwards and downwards rather than sideways. Sometimes a party in full swing above or below can be a nuisance – especially if you have not been invited, and clogs on an uncarpeted floor may disturb your dreams, but such things are comparatively rare.

The questions all seekers after the sun ask are, "What do

properties cost in Spain today?" and "How much house for how much money?" There is such a variety of properties available all over the country that one cannot be precise. Only a few years ago most Spanish properties were extremely cheap, but since then prices have escalated, sometimes by as much as forty per cent in a year. In the country, away from the tourist areas, there are still good bargains to be found, and even on the coast prices compare very favourably with Britain. In the big cities such as Madrid, Barcelona and Seville, prices are of course high.

In the spring of 1979 I went to find out about prices on the Costa del Sol and visited a brand new development on the Mijas-Costa between Marbella and Fuengirola. Here there was a large range of houses built on a pleasant wooded slope just north of the main coast road. Unlike the isolated development I mentioned earlier, this one had been planned with a large variety of different types of dwellings with every possible amenity, from hard tennis-courts, riding-stables, a community centre and a school, to two new hotels, a church and a supermarket. It had a number of green zones, and across the main road a private beach. The only thing missing was a golf-course, but there are many along this part of the coast only a short drive away.

What does property cost here? I was first shown an unusual building consisting of three small houses on two floors, which I suppose one could describe as a "triplex". There will eventually be fifteen dwellings in five separate blocks sharing their own garden and swimming-pool. They were well designed and built to a high standard. On the ground floor was a reasonably large sitting/dining-room and kitchen, and upstairs were two double bedrooms and bathroom with lavatory. By clever design all this had been contained in about 75 square metres. They were attractive houses for a holiday but lacked storage-space for a permanent home. Instead of two bedrooms, some have one large bedroom and a dressing-room with a good built-in cupboard, and this could be lived in all the year round. The price of these dwellings was £21,000, of which half can be paid on possession and the balance over two years plus bank interest. For about £2,000 more, the developers will provide all furniture and furnishings.

Further up the hill, well away from the main road, are separate villas in individual plots of 600 square metres. They come in three sizes. The smallest has a floor area of 75 square metres with 27 square metres of terraces. On one floor, with sloping tiled roofs, it contains a reasonably-sized living-room, two small double bedrooms, kitchen and bathroom. The next has a bigger split-level living-room and two larger bedrooms. The floor area is 94 square metres with 20 square metres of terraces. In addition there is a patio for sun-bathing, over the bedrooms, which is reached by an outside staircase. Finally, the largest villas have a third bedroom and second bathroom on the first floor. The total area including terraces and patio in this style is 141 square metres. All of these villas are most attractive, and they are priced respectively at £24,000, £34,300 and £37,800.

In another zone it is planned to build what the developers call an "English Garden Estate". There will be twenty-one houses, each with small gardens of about a sixth of an acre surrounding a large communal garden with swimming-pool. Here is a chance to mow a lawn without a trip to England.

Made in English-style bricks painted white, with mullioned windows and dark brown tiled roofs, these houses will be offered in three sizes. For £35,000 you will get a sitting-room, dining-room, two large bedrooms, kitchen, bathroom and cloak-room. £43,750 will buy an extra bedroom and bathroom, and for £52,500 you will have a really impressive house with four bedrooms, three bathrooms and a large sun-bathing terrace on the roof.

Considering their favoured position overlooking the Mediterranean, these houses are good value today, and all fittings will be guaranteed for six months and the building for ten years.

There are a large number of similar developments at comparable prices all along the Costa del Sol. As soon as one gets sold up, another starts. Prices on the east coast tend to be slightly less, but even on the Costa del Sol there are quite a number of small flats being built for under £14,000.

In the spring of 1979 one could buy new studio flats for only £8,000, flats with one bedroom from £9,600, and with two bedrooms from £13,250. New houses with similar accommodation generally cost about twice as much.

Many bargains can be found among the properties for re-sale. Some on offer at the present time are as follows:

FLATS		
Fuengirola	One bedroom, fully furnished	£9,200
	Two bedrooms	£12,800
	Two bedrooms, large sun-terrace, near town centre and fully furnished	£13,000
Los Boliches	Two bedrooms, fully furnished	£11,100
Marbella	One bedroom, fully furnished	£11,500
	One bedroom, fully furnished, on sea front	£16,000
HOUSES		
Mijas-Costa	Two bedrooms, fully furnished	£38,000
	One bedroom, fully furnished, large sun-terrace with sea view	£25,700
	One bedroom, fully furnished, 50 yards from beach	£20,010
	Two bedrooms, fully furnished	£33,000
Marbella	Pueblo-type town houses, one or two bedrooms	£20/26,000
	Three bedrooms, two bathrooms, in country	£35,000

Marbella	One bedroom, fully furnished, 50 yards from beach in country	£13,800
	Town house, two bedrooms, fully furnished	£16,000

In many cases these prices are negotiable downwards, and extended payments are sometimes available. By searching around, one can find even better bargains that are not advertised, particularly in the country a few kilometres inland.

As all prices continue to rise, it is best to buy early before you come to live in Spain. The Investment Currency Premium is no longer payable.

CHAPTER 3

Buying Property

Having found a delightful villa or flat in your favourite part of Spain, with just the right accommodation, in beautiful surroundings and, above all, at a price you can afford, you are naturally impatient to take possession of your new home. This is the moment to proceed with caution.

Buying a house or flat is quite different from buying a piece of furniture or a television set. It is not just a question of a quick inspection, paying the price and carrying it away under your arm. So many problems can arise in the purchase of property – problems that cannot be seen by the closest inspection, and only a lawyer can protect you from making a bad investment – and for many it is the most important investment of their lives. The lawyer is your guarantee that you will get what you are paying for.

Let us consider what happens in England. You instruct a solicitor to act on your behalf, and the first thing he does is to arrange with the vendor's solicitor for an agreement for sale to be drawn up and signed by both parties. This agreement sets out in detail the terms of the transaction. It describes the property and its boundaries, and what fixtures and fittings are to be included. The purchase price is stated and when it will be payable, and the vendor undertakes to give you vacant possession by a certain date.

There will be special provisions to protect you as purchaser, such as a right to cancel the agreement if some vital and irremovable problem should arise before the transaction is completed. If the house is yet to be built, then further clauses will be necessary to protect the purchaser. The agreement for sale is a most important document.

But that is not all that a purchaser's solicitor does. He has to make many searches and enquiries to protect the interests of his client. He will inspect the Land Registry to make sure that the seller is the true owner and has power to sell, that he is not bankrupt and that there are no onerous obligations imposed on the owner of the property. He will want to know if there is a mortgage to be paid off before completion of the sale.

Next the solicitor will make searches in the local Land Registries to find out if there are any charges registered against the property. These may include private street and improvement expenses, building lines, housing restrictions and compulsory purchase orders, and there may be many other matters of concern to a prospective owner, who does not want to find in a few years' time that a new motorway is to be constructed at the bottom of his garden, or that his house is to be demolished to make way for a new housing estate. Are the boundaries of the property clearly defined? Have the neighbours rights of support or rights of way? If the new owner wishes to let, has a maximum permissible rent been registered with the local rent officer? The purchaser's solicitor wants to know the answers to all these questions.

In Britain people often complain about the legal expense involved in buying and selling property. These complaints arise through a lack of understanding as to what a solicitor does, and the time and skill he employs to protect his client.

As in Britain, so in Spain, a qualified lawyer is essential when buying property. Remember that you will be buying in a foreign country where the laws are different and the documents worded in a foreign language. As a United Kingdom resident you may also require the services of a British lawyer.

In Spain all sales and purchases of real property, which includes land as well as buildings or parts of buildings, have to be recorded in a local register, and the conveyance deed, called an *Escritura de compraventa*, is drawn up by a lawyer appointed by the local authority. He is known as a *notario*, and his duties are to see that the property is properly described in the deed, that the 'official' purchase price has been paid to the seller and, when the fees and taxes have been met, that the property is registered in the name of the new owner in the local property register.

If the property is being bought from a Spanish National or a Spanish Company, or even from a foreigner who is resident in Spain, the *notario* will need to be satisfied – by seeing a bank certificate – that the 'official' price (the price stated in the *Escritura*) has been paid into a Spanish bank account. The deed must be signed by both the seller and the purchaser, or their legally appointed agents, in his presence.

Because these functions are carried out by an experienced *notario*, it is often said that there is no need for a purchaser in Spain to instruct a Spanish lawyer. It is strictly true that property can be bought without the assistance of a lawyer, but it is extremely unwise for a United Kingdom resident not to have an *abogado*, the equivalent of an English solicitor, to watch his interests. There are as many things that can go wrong in Spain as in Britain. You will have to pay the *abogado*'s fees, but it will be well worth it. To buy a property without legal assistance is to be 'penny wise and pound foolish'.

It is also important, before you commit yourself, to find out what financial obligations you will be undertaking. Apart from rates and taxes there may well be other annual expenses. It often happens in Spain – particularly on the coast – that properties are part of a development of several houses, or flats in a block of apartments. If this is so, there will be contributions payable to the Association of Owners for the upkeep of the communal garden, the maintenance of the swimming-pool, repairing and insuring the buildings, paying the wages of a handyman, a porter or a guard, and so on.

Ask to see the regulations of the community, the *Estatutos de la Comunidad*, and read them carefully. If you do not fully understand them, discuss them with the Chairman of the Association of Owners, *el Presidente*, the Administrator or your *abogado*, and use a friend as interpreter if necessary.

Having satisfied yourself on these matters, the next thing is to go and see your *abogado* – in most large towns there are several who speak English. Ask him to search at the local deed registry to find out if the seller is registered as the true owner and can make good title to the property, and instruct him to prepare an agreement for sale. If there is a standard form used in a development, your *abogado* will approve it on your behalf and see that your interests are protected.

If your *abogado* advises that everything is in order, then you may sign the agreement for sale. If you pay a deposit, make sure that it will be returned in the event of non-completion of the purchase through the fault of the seller.

Now that British Exchange Control has been abolished, you can pay a deposit out of your holiday money. Bank of England permission is no longer required and no Investment Currency Premium is payable. Your British Bank will provide the necessary pesetas to complete the purchase.

Under Spanish law the *Escritura*, the formal deed of conveyance, has to be signed by both the seller and the purchaser in the presence of the *notario*. If it is not convenient for you to return to Spain for this purpose, then you can appoint someone to appear before the *notario* and sign on your behalf. He can be your *abogado* or a friend who lives in Spain, and he need not be a Spanish National. He must, however, be appointed by a deed, which in England would be called a 'Special Power of Attorney', and in Spain an '*Escritura de poder de compraventa.*'

The deed can be drawn up by the Spanish Embassy in London, but this takes time as it has to be authenticated in Madrid before it can be used. It is much quicker – and cheaper – to have the deed prepared by the *notario* himself as soon as you have agreed to buy your house or flat. Leave it with your *abogado* or friend, who can then arrange to sign the Conveyance Deed as soon as you tell him that you have obtained the necessary pesetas. There is one important point to watch. If the Spanish property is to be registered in the names of a husband and wife, then the Power of Attorney must state that the agent has power to sign on behalf of both parties.

Soon after the *Escritura* is signed, the fees and stamp duty are payable, and then the property will be registered. The original deed will be held at the property register, but you can have an official copy.

Finally, often many months later, there will be a tax payable on the increase in the value of the property since its previous transfer, similar to the British Capital Gains Tax.

There are two fees, one for the preparation of the *Escritura* and the other for its registration. The amount of these fees varies from one district to another. The stamp duty is charged at 8·4 per cent of the 'official value', and the Capital Gains Tax at twenty-five per cent of the increase in such value since the previous transfer, whether by conveyance or by inheritance. If there has been no increase in that period, the tax charged will be ten per cent of the amount paid on the previous transfer.

It is the normal practice for the seller to pay the fees for the preparation of the *Escritura* and the Capital Gains Tax. This tax has the impressive name of the '*arbitrio sobre incremento del valor de los terrenos*' ('the tax on the increase in the value of land') but this is shortened to the more convenient name of '*plus valia*'. The purchaser normally pays the registration fees and the stamp duty, the '*impuestos de transmisiones*'. However, this practice can be altered by mutual agreement. Sometimes the purchaser is asked to pay all fees and taxes, and in this case the agreement for sale will state that he is to pay '*todos gastos*', 'all expenses'.

It is not possible to give any accurate estimate as to the total amount of these fees and taxes. Not only do the notarial fees vary but the amount of the *plus valia* depends on how long a period has elapsed since the previous transfer. In the average case one should allow between ten and fifteen per cent of the 'official value'. A few years ago it was just over thirteen per cent when I purchased. If, however, the seller has owned the property for many years, the *plus valia* could be a substantial amount. Your *abogado* will be able to advise on this.

One thing that surprises British buyers is that the purchase price mentioned in the *Escritura* is nearly always far less than the actual price being paid. Do not worry. There is nothing illegal about this, and it is common practice all over Spain. Every property has a registered 'official value', and this is the figure entered in the *Escritura*, and on which the fees and taxes are calculated. It can be compared with the 'rateable value' in England, and every few years is re-assessed – upwards of course.

If you want the *Escritura* to state the full purchase price – after all, there is a bit of Anglo-Saxon in many of us – then discuss the matter with your *abogado*. He will probably advise against trying to alter the normal custom. In Spain it seldom pays to 'step out of line', and it can lead to considerable frustration and unexpected expenses. The agreement for sale will state the actual purchase price.

For the British purchaser this practice has both advantages and disadvantages. It means that both fees and taxes are lower, but on the other hand it has the disadvantage that it will limit the amount you can borrow on mortgage, and also the amount you can take out of Spain if you decide to sell and return to Britain. This is more fully explained in Chapter 11.

It may be suggested by your friends in Spain that you do not really need an *Escritura* to become the owner of your property, and that you can safely rely on a private agreement for sale. It is true that in the past properties have frequently changed hands without an *Escritura*, with the object no doubt of saving fees and taxes, but no United Kingdom resident should ever agree to this. An *Escritura* is always essential.

Article 1280 of the Civil Code lays down that the purchase of real property in Spain must be completed by an *Escritura* which is signed by both parties (or their agents appointed by deed) in the presence of a *notario*, and the *Escritura* must then be registered in the name of the purchaser in the local deed registry.

The legal position as to private agreements for sale is set out in Articles 1278 and 1279 of the Civil Code. Such agreements create an effective contractual relationship between the parties, enabling either to compel the other to appear before a *notario* to execute an *Escritura* as soon as the full purchase price is paid or tendered.

To rely on a private agreement only, however, is dangerous for a purchaser for the following reasons.

1 The seller might at any time sell to a third party under an *Escritura*, and as soon as the property was registered in the name of such third party he would become the true owner, and the rights of the original purchaser would be extinguished.
2 The seller might mortgage the property without the purchaser's knowledge, and as soon as the mortgage was registered the mortgagee's rights over the property would have priority over those of the purchaser.
3 The seller might become insolvent, and his secured creditors on registering their claims would have the first right to the property.
4 In rural areas in the Balearics, the Canaries and in certain parts of mainland Spain, which have been declared special areas for strategic or defence purposes, a private agreement has no legal effect at all if the purchaser is not a Spanish National. The only way a British subject can become an owner of a property in these parts is by an *Escritura* which records the permission of the Army Ministry. (Article 1 of 12th May 1960, Decree

dated 10th February 1978, and Article 21 of the Foreign Investment Regulations.)

Therefore always insist on having an *Escritura* signed and registered in your name.

The restrictions on owning properties in strategic and defence areas are important. First, the total area that may be owned by foreign individuals (that is, other than Spanish Nationals) and foreign companies in any of the Spanish islands may not exceed twenty-five per cent of the total area of any one of them. Secondly, in certain small areas of mainland Spain rural properties cannot be owned by foreigners without the permission of the Army Ministry. These mainland areas are the Campo de Gibraltar, parts of Galicia, Cartagena, Chafarinas, Alhucemas and the Peñón de Vélez de la Gomera.

The part most likely to concern British emigrants is the Campo de Gibraltar, which extends from the Guadiaro river on the east to just beyond Tarifa on the west and for some 20 kilometres inland.

These restrictions date back as far as 1935, but in December 1936 they were modified by a new law which stated that permission would be granted to foreigners wishing to own rural properties in centres declared to be of 'national tourist interest'. Sotogrande in the Campo de Gibraltar is one of the best known of these centres. Outside these centres permission is not usually granted, though I have been told that it is sometimes given to suitable applicants where relatively small properties are involved.

In a few of these restricted areas it has become the practice for British people to have their rural properties registered in the names of Spanish Nationals as 'nominees'. Not only is this against the law (for which you can be fined up to 500,000 pesetas and have the property expropriated) but you have no legal rights at all in the property.

Under British law a trustee can be compelled to deal with property in accordance with the wishes of the beneficial owner, but in Spain it is different. Under Spanish law the so-called 'nominee' is the true and only owner, and any agreement he may make with you either verbally or in writing will be of no effect. On his death the property will belong to the beneficiaries under his Will or to his next-of-kin according to the Spanish laws of succession.

So, if you wish to live in one of these restricted areas, and fail to get permission to own a property in the country, then choose a house or flat in a 'tourist centre', or in an *urbanización* (a town or large village and their suburbs) where there are no such restrictions.

Apart from these few and comparatively small strategic and defence areas, there are restrictions on foreigners owning large plots of land. Express government permission is required to buy more than four hectares (9·88 acres) of irrigated rural land or twenty hectares (49·42 acres) if it is not irrigated, and such permission is seldom forthcoming. This will not, however, concern British emigrants – unless of course they are planning to take up farming in Spain.

In addition, if you want to buy a building-site for the erection of more than one house for your personal use, or the total area exceeds five thousand square metres (1·23 acres), it is treated as a 'business activity' and will require special permission from the Director General of Foreign Transactions.

At first sight these restrictions and regulations may appear rather formidable, but they will apply to only a very few who intend to live in Spain. Provided that you have a Spanish lawyer watching your interests, there should be no problems. He will keep you right.

Some may wish to have a mortgage to buy a Spanish property. You can raise the money in Britain, provided the security for the loan is a British property or British stocks and shares. It is unlikely that your local Building Society will be very interested, but Banks, Insurance Societies and other financial institutions can often help.

Many property developers provide loans or allow extended payments. One large development I know on the

Costa del Sol offers British buyers three choices. They can pay cash in full on signing the contract and get a five per cent discount, pay by three equal instalments over two years and lose the discount, or pay forty per cent of the price and the balance over a period of five years by half-yearly instalments. In this latter case interest will, of course, be charged every six months on the outstanding balance, but it will probably be at a lower rate than is usual in Britain.

Unfortunately there is no equivalent in Spain to a British Building Society, but in July 1975 a new law was passed which in certain cases allows a United Kingdom resident to obtain a loan from a Spanish bank for the purchase of Spanish real estate. The following conditions must be satisfied:

1 Permission must be obtained from the Director General of Foreign Transactions.
2 The loan must be for the purchase of a newly constructed property from a Spanish National resident in Spain.
3 The terms of the loan must not be more favourable than those relating to ordinary loans to Spanish residents.
4 Repayment must be in foreign currency or 'convertible' pesetas.
5 The mortgage must be secured on the specific property in question.

Once you are living in Spain as a permanent resident, you can, of course, obtain a loan from your Spanish bank without any special conditions in the same way as a Spanish National, provided the bank manager considers you creditworthy.

There is a lot to be said for buying your house or flat well ahead of your emigration. Starting a new life in a foreign country naturally involves a lot of planning, and it will be a great relief to know that your future home is already yours – just waiting for you to move in. Also you will be able to buy for less, as property prices in Spain are continually rising; although I am glad to say that in the vast majority of cases they are nothing like as high as in Britain.

Until you emigrate, you can let your property and obtain a good return on your investment, particularly in the summer months in the tourist areas. You must, however, be careful that your tenant does not become protected against eviction. The Spanish laws about this are explained in the next chapter.

Once you have become the owner of a Spanish property, it is essential to have someone who lives in Spain to look after it until you emigrate, and see to paying all necessary expenses.

There will be rates and taxes payable. These are called respectively '*Contribuciones Urbana*' and '*Derechos y Tasas Sobre la Propriedad Inmueble*'. In some Provinces they are payable twice a year, in others only once. Normally no demands are sent out as in Britain, and there are fines of twenty per cent if they are not paid on time. There may also be quarterly contributions due to the Association of Owners of a community or block of flats. Electricity and water accounts must be paid promptly or these services will be cut off. If there is a telephone, the accounts are usually presented every two months, and the National Telephone Company is quick to cut you off if there is any undue delay in payment. It costs a lot to have a telephone reconnected, and it may take many months if by then there is no free line available.

Your Spanish bank may be prepared to meet all these expenses – some can be relied on, but some cannot. But a bank will not be prepared to inspect your property, deal with essential repairs or arrange lettings. For these matters you need a reliable agent, and in the case of lettings someone who knows the law.

If your house or flat is part of a community, the President or Administrator may be willing to act as your agent. If not, you may have a British or American friend living permanently in Spain who can help you.

Failing all else, you should instruct a reliable *gestor* or one of the professional property managers, *agentes de inmuebles*, who exist in Spain. A *gestor* has no exact counterpart in Britain. He is a specialist who does many things that would normally be handled by an accountant, a solicitor, a civil servant or a Citizen's Advice Bureau. He is, in fact, an administrator who can cope with many financial problems and some legal matters, and above all is an expert at completing the multiplicity of documents that so often turn up in Spain. When you come to live in Spain, you will certainly need the services of a *gestor*, and if you already know a good one, he can look after your affairs while you are still living in Britain. You will have to pay for the services of a *gestor* or a property manager, but he will save you considerable trouble and unnecessary expense.

To sum up, here are six golden rules for the United Kingdom resident who is buying his first property in Spain.

1 Instruct a qualified Spanish lawyer to watch your interests.
2 Before agreeing to buy, consider the obligations you will be undertaking as the owner of a Spanish property.
3 Do not rely on a private agreement for sale, but insist on an *Escritura*, signed and registered in your name.
4 Do not have the property registered in the name of a Spanish 'nominee'.
5 Make sure that your 'foreign money contribution', that is, the amount of pesetas purchased by Sterling, is recorded in the Property Register and the Foreign Investment Register (see Chapter 11).
6 Appoint a reliable agent to look after your property and pay all expenses until you emigrate.

These are the things to remember when buying property – your first and most important step towards a happy future in Spain.

N. B above.

CHAPTER 4

Letting Property

The new owner of a house or flat in Spain, whether it has been bought as a future home or only for annual holidays, may want to let it. It has probably cost him an appreciable amount of capital, and he should have some return on his investment.

Also there will be taxes to be met. Each year rates and taxes fall due, also water charges. Possibly contributions to an Association of Owners and mortgage repayments will have to be met as well. It makes economic sense to let.

The two most important things to remember about letting property are to choose the tenants with the greatest care and generally to have an agreement in writing.

Nothing makes up for a bad tenant. A new house or flat can soon deteriorate if it is not looked after carefully. Much of the rent can disappear in paying for repairs to both the property and its furniture and furnishings. You may have difficulty in getting a tenant out at the end of his tenancy, or he may make a 'moonlight flit' with the rent unpaid. You should, of course, always take the rent in advance.

Except in the case of a British tenant who takes the property for a short holiday of a few weeks, you should always have a signed tenancy agreement. Beware of the potential tenant who says, "Don't bother about any written agreement. We will shake hands and leave it as a 'gentlemen's agreement' – there will be no problems." In my experience a 'gentleman' is always prepared to put his signature to what he has agreed.

There is another reason for a written agreement. With the passage of time it is easy to forget what was originally decided. Recently two friends of mine fell out over the letting of a flat. They were both intelligent and responsible people, but the tenant thought the rent included the use of the garage, and the landlord was certain that it had been agreed that an additional rent would be payable for the garage. A written agreement would have prevented this misunderstanding.

If possible, arrange the letting of your future home yourself, but if you have to leave it to a friend, be certain that he will watch your interests and look after the property as if it were his own.

An agreement for letting can be quite a simple document but it should deal with the following matters:

1 The amount of the rent and the manner in which it should be paid. It is usual in Spain for rent to be paid monthly in advance.
2 The precise period of the letting. For reasons I shall explain later, this should be for less than one year, and not for an indefinite period, such as from month to month. If you want to let for more than a year, and the tenant has proved satisfactory, have another agreement signed at the end of eleven months.
3 The articles of furniture, furnishings, linen and crockery etc. included in the letting should be specified, and the tenant should agree to replace or pay for any damaged or lost articles. It is often wise to have a separate inventory of the contents signed by both parties. This protects both landlord and tenant.
4 The responsibility for such expenses as electricity and gas consumed during the tenancy should also be stated. For short periods they are sometimes included in the rent, but generally it is better for the tenant to undertake to pay for these items in addition to the rent. Read the

electricity meter at the beginning and end of the tenancy. See that the tenant starts with full gas cylinders and leaves full cylinders when he departs.

Electricity accounts often arrive many weeks after the period they cover, and long after the tenant has gone, so calculate the cost of the electricity consumed by multiplying the number of units used by the average price per unit shown on the previous account. Even in Spain a family can spend £15 or more each month on electricity in the winter, particularly if there is an automatic washing-machine.

5 The tenant should undertake to pay the cost of any damage or loss that may occur during the tenancy to the interior of the building, its fittings or its contents.

Sometimes it is wise to take a deposit from the tenant against such eventuality and return it to him at the end of the tenancy, having deducted the cost of any repairs or replacements.

6 The tenant should agree not to sublet the property or assign the tenancy without the written permission of the landlord. Many other matters can be covered by an agreement, but these are the important ones.

The agreement should be written in Spanish, unless the tenant is English-speaking, and it is wise to have it prepared by a Spanish lawyer. There should be two copies signed, one for the landlord and one for the tenant.

If there is a telephone in your property, a tenant can land you with considerable expense. His teenaged daughter may have a boy friend on the other side of the world – and young love has no sense of time. Do not have the telephone cut off, because re-connection will involve trouble, delay and expense. The solution is to go to a Spanish ironmonger's, a *ferretería*, and buy an ingenious little gadget which can be locked on the dial. It should cost you under £1. It permits incoming calls but prevents a tenant making out-going calls.

Letting a Spanish property for an indefinite period, or for a fixed period of a year or more, involves the risk of being landed with a tenant who is protected by law against eviction. As in Britain, so in Spain, tenants have to be protected against arbitrary eviction from their homes and excessive increases in rent. The landlord also needs protection against a bad tenant who does not pay his rent or lets the property deteriorate.

The Spanish law on this subject is contained in the *Ley de Arrendiamentos Urbanos*, the Law of Urban Lettings. Like the Landlord and Tenant Acts in Britain, this statute is complicated and has 152 sections and several schedules, and it is possible to give only a summary of its provisions. If you do get landed with this problem, you will need the help of a Spanish lawyer.

This law does not, however, apply when you let your house or flat to a tenant in consequence of his employment with you, or when the letting is for a short and fixed period, such as a summer holiday. In these cases the tenant has to rely on his rights under the tenancy agreement. He can stay in the property for the period mentioned, so long as he pays the rent and does not break any express conditions of the agreement, but after that he must leave.

In general the *Ley de Arrendiamentos Urbanos* applies to all lettings of private houses or flats for an indefinite period or for a fixed period of one year or more (whether furniture is included or not). It is the indefinite period that catches many people out. Beware of the prospective tenant who says that he wants to stay for only a few months and that he will pay the rent monthly in advance. Unless he signs an agreement for a fixed period of less than a year, he has the protection of Spanish Law against eviction from the moment he moves in and pays the first month's rent.

In Spain a protected tenant has three basic rights. His rent is controlled; his tenancy can be terminated only for certain specified reasons; and at the end of any stated period of the tenancy (if it is for a year or longer), he has the right to have the period extended, subject to certain exceptions that I will mention later.

The amount of rent that can be charged is controlled in the following manner. If the house or flat has been built with financial help from the Government, either by way of a loan or by an outright grant, then the Government fixes the maximum rent that can be charged. However, when it has been built without such help, the landlord can charge whatever rent he can get. Once there is a tenant his rent can be increased only by amounts authorized by law. Each year the Government declares the permitted percentage increase in accordance with the official rise in the cost of living.

The landlord can terminate a protected tenancy before the end of the period stated in the agreement and apply to the Court for an Order for possession when the tenant has committed any of the following offences.

1 He has failed to pay the rent. If, however, he has failed because he is out of work, the Court will give him time to pay before making any order for possession.
2 He has unlawfully sublet the property. A subletting is always unlawful in the case of furnished premises, and also in the case of unfurnished premises without the landlord's consent, or if there are more than two subtenants and the landlord has not been informed within thirty days of the subletting together with the names of the subtenants.
3 He has sublet for more than the legally authorized rent.
4 He has assigned the tenancy without the landlord's written consent.
5 He has converted the property into business premises without the landlord's consent. An example of this would be changing a residential property into a shop or factory. However, if a tenant carries on some private work, such as painting or writing or giving language lessons to a few students, this would not amount to a conversion to business premises which would entitle a landlord to terminate the tenancy.

6 He has caused serious damage to the property or made unauthorized alterations.
7 He is using the property for immoral purposes, has created a danger or is causing serious nuisance or annoyance to adjoining occupiers.

In addition to his rights of a controlled rent and protection against arbitrary eviction, a tenant (who has a tenancy for a fixed period of one year or more) is also entitled to an extension of his tenancy for a further period. The tenant cannot waive this right. Any condition in a tenancy agreement that the tenant shall not be entitled to an extension is of no effect.

However, the law looks after the interests of the landlord as well, and lays down certain cases when he is entitled to refuse an extension and regain possession of his property. These are some of them:

1 If the landlord is living near the property and requires possession for his own occupation or the occupation of members of his family. In the case of a British resident, who wants to live in his house or flat on his retirement to Spain, the Court could refuse to allow the tenant an extension of the tenancy provided that the principle of reciprocity exists. This principle is a fundamental concept of Spanish law. It means that, in general, a foreigner will be granted the same legal rights in Spain as a Spanish National would be granted in the foreigner's own country.

   In Britain a landlord can ask for an order for possession on the grounds that he requires to occupy the property himself, and a Spanish National owning property in Britain would have the same right. Therefore if you have let your Spanish house or flat to a tenant for a fixed period of a year or more, you can at the end of that period refuse an extension of the tenancy, because you want to live in it.
2 If the landlord lives in the same town as the property and wants to live there because an increase in his family

has made his existing home over-crowded.

3 If the landlord has married and requires the property for his matrimonial home.
4 If the tenant or his family does not occupy the property for more than six months a year. However, this will not be a ground for refusing an extension of the tenancy if the tenant has a justifiable reason for his absence, such as military service or work outside Spain.
5 If the tenant occupies other houses or flats in the same locality without good reason, such as the size of his family.
6 If the tenant has alternative accommodation which is suitable for the needs of himself and his family.

We find, therefore, that in Spain the position is very much the same as in Britain, but there are differences in procedure.

A tenant who wishes to exercise the right to an extension of his tenancy must give the landlord a written notice at least thirty days before the end of the original period, and if a landlord wishes to refuse the extension, he must then give the tenant twelve months' notice, giving his reasons. Such a notice must be sent by a *notario*, so that later it can be proved that the tenant received it.

A tenant who gives up possession of a property at the expiration of a twelve months' notice is entitled to a refund of a year's rent, provided, of course, he has paid it since receiving the notice. If he continues in the property, then he forfeits his right to any refund, and the landlord can apply to the Court for an Order that the tenant should vacate the property within four months.

When a tenant dies, Spanish law gives protection to his family. A wife (who is not separated from her husband) becomes the tenant and has the same right to an extension. If there is no wife, then other members of the tenant's family are protected. They include children, parents, grandparents and even brothers and sisters, provided that they have lived with the tenant in the property for at least two years before his death.

In this chapter I have set out some of the grounds which entitle the owner of a Spanish house or flat to terminate a tenancy or to refuse an extension of the original period, but the existence of such grounds does not mean that he will automatically get possession. The Court, as in Britain, has a discretion to decide whether or not the tenant must leave. It has to take into account the balance of hardship. In such cases both parties are suffering hardship – the owner because he needs possession of his property, and the tenant because he has to find a new home for himself and his family. The Court has to decide which of them is suffering the greater hardship.

A point that is not often appreciated is that not only Spanish tenants are protected against eviction and excessive increases in rent but also other nationalities, when reciprocity exists between their country and Spain. In Britain a Spanish tenant is protected by law, and so a British tenant will be protected by these Spanish laws. It does not matter whether he has a Residence Permit or not. He will be protected if he actually lives in Spain and is not just on holiday.

Therefore, if you can avoid it, do not let your property in Spain for a period of a year or more, or for an indefinite period. On the other hand, if you do not need to live in the property for several years, and have a particularly good tenant who lives in Spain and looks after your property well, you may wish to let it to him for a long period.

Most British owners, of course, let for fixed periods of less than a year and therefore will not be concerned with these laws. Before we came to live permanently in Spain, we often let our flat to both British and Spanish tenants and had no problems.

CHAPTER 5

Saving Tax

When you leave Britain to live permanently in Spain, it will affect your liability to taxes in both countries. It is a matter to be considered carefully when making your financial plans, and one on which you will need expert advice from an accountant, and probably from a stockbroker as well.

In a book of this sort it is possible only to illustrate some of the factors that will affect your tax position, and it is necessary to consider both British and Spanish tax laws.

A BRITISH TAX

Income tax is charged to a British resident on all his income after deduction of certain reliefs and allowances.

The June 1979 Budget makes the following proposals for the tax year 1979–80. Personal reliefs will be increased to £1,165 for a single person and £1,815 for a married couple. For those over retirement age (sixty-five for a man, sixty for a woman), they will be increased to £1,540 and £2,455 respectively, provided total income does not exceed £5,000. Additional reliefs will be given for a wife's earned income up to £1,165, Life Assurance premiums, dependent relatives etc.

After deduction of the appropriate reliefs, the remainder of one's income is taxed at twenty-five per cent on the first £750, and thereafter at a basic rate of thirty per cent up to £10,000 a year. Over that amount of income the rates of tax increase to a maximum of sixty per cent over £25,000. The Investment Income Surcharge will be at a single rate of fifteen per cent on incomes over £5,000.

This Budget has dramatically reduced the burden of income tax for those who live in Britain, and in consequence the tax saving for those who emigrate to Spain is now less than it was. The present rates of Spanish income tax are, however, still much lower than the British, and most people who emigrate to Spain will find their total tax bill considerably lightened, as I shall demonstrate later in this chapter.

The first thing to appreciate is that liability to pay income tax depends on two factors – where you live, and your source of income. In general terms, British income tax is payable in the following cases.

1 On all income, wherever it arises, when it belongs to a person who is resident for tax purposes in the United Kingdom.
2 On income arising in the United Kingdom only, when it belongs to a person who for tax purposes is not resident in the United Kingdom.

First it is necessary to consider what is meant by being resident in the United Kingdom for tax purposes. The British tax year runs from 6th April in one year to 5th April in the following year. Anyone who is physically present in the United Kingdom for a period, or periods, amounting to six months or more in a particular tax year is resident in the United Kingdom for that tax year. This is strictly interpreted as being 183 days in the tax year (and an extra day is not allowed in a leap year). In practice the day of arrival and day of departure is ignored. There is no exception to this rule. If you catch influenza on the 182nd day and leave for Spain two days later, it is just too bad. For that tax year you are resident in the United Kingdom and become liable to pay British tax on your whole income, from whatever country it comes.

There are two cases when a person may be considered as resident in the United Kingdom for purposes of income tax even when he has been absent for more than 182 days. These are first, if he lives permanently abroad but has accommodation available for his use in the United Kingdom and pays a visit, however short, in a tax year, and secondly, even if he has no such accommodation available but pays "habitual and substantial visits" to the United Kingdom.

"Accommodation available for his use" means accommodation which is in fact available for his use, whether he owns it or not. Having a permanent arrangement for use of a room in someone else's house or in an hotel would be treated as "available accommodation". On the other hand, owning a house that is let on a long lease with no right to possession would not. Accommodation rented for use during a temporary stay will also not be considered "available for use", provided the total period of the renting does not exceed two years for furnished accommodation and one year if unfurnished.

In the case of someone working full time abroad, accommodation in the United Kingdom owned by him (or rented on a long lease) will not be treated as "available for his use" provided the work is carried on wholly abroad, and he does not own (and is not a partner in) a business which has a branch or permanent establishment in the United Kingdom.

"Accommodation available for the use" of a wife will normally be treated as available for the husband, and *vice versa.*

The second case when a person will be considered as resident in the United Kingdom for tax purposes is when he makes 'substantial' visits though they do not amount to 183 days in a tax year. Visits are regarded as 'substantial' when they amount in total to an average of three months or more each year over a period of four consecutive years.

Anyone who emigrates to Spain and makes it his permanent home will not normally be treated as resident in the United Kingdom and will therefore be charged British Tax only on income arising in Britain. Unless you are working full time in Spain, be careful not to have accommodation "available for your use" in Britain, and do not spend on average more than three months there every year.

It takes some time before you will be treated as not resident for tax purposes. The tax authorities have to be satisfied that your decision to live in Spain is genuine and likely to be permanent. Normally they will not make a final decision as to this until at least one full tax year has passed since you left Britain. If you emigrate in June 1980, for example, a final decision will not be made until after 5th April 1982. They will also require some evidence that your permanent home is in Spain, such as the sale of your house in Britain and the purchase of a house or flat in Spain.

Once the tax authorities are satisfied that you are "not resident and not ordinarily resident" in the United Kingdom, you will cease to be liable to British tax on any foreign income from the actual date of your emigration, and any tax already paid or suffered on such income will be repaid to you.

Some people have got the idea that they must stay out of Britain for a full tax year before they will be considered as "not resident and not ordinarily resident". This is not so. They can return on holiday whenever they like without prejudicing their tax position (but such holidays must not exceed a total of 182 days).

Once you have been designated as "not resident and not ordinarily resident" in the United Kingdom, you will continue to be treated as such, provided you do not (a) visit Britain for periods amounting to 183 days or more in any tax year, (b) take average visits of three months a year for four years in succession, and (c) have accommodation "available for your use" (unless you are working full time in Spain).

Remember also that for tax purposes a husband and wife are normally treated as one person, so watch those visits. If your wife has a lengthy stay with her elderly aunt in Britain, it could cost you a lot of extra tax that year.

Although living permanently in Spain, you will still remain liable to tax on income arising in the United Kingdom, but there is one important exception to this: the interest on certain British Government Stocks is treated as 'foreign income' and therefore free of tax for those who have emigrated to live abroad. In Appendix II there is a list of those Government Stocks which at the present time are free of tax to persons "not ordinarily resident" in the United Kingdom.

Apart from 3½ per cent War Stock and four per cent Victory Bonds, these are all 'dated' stocks, so that when they are redeemed you will normally receive more than they cost. The effect of inflation – which now seems a permanent feature of every European country – will have depreciated their real value, but on the other hand their income yield is usually much higher than can be obtained on ordinary stocks and shares. With the added advantage of being free of tax, this means that spending income can be increased considerably, which is an important consideration to many emigrants to Spain. When an individual can finally be regarded as "not ordinarily resident in the United Kingdom," it can be arranged for the interest on such Government Stocks to be paid gross, thus saving the trouble and delay of reclaiming the tax each year.

Any other income arising in the United Kingdom, such as company dividends, rents and pensions, is normally subject to British income tax, but there are a few exceptions. I would advise you to discuss your particular circumstances with a qualified accountant.

Once you are "not resident and not ordinarily resident in the United Kingdom", you can avoid British tax by investing in foreign stocks and shares, but do be careful that they are really foreign. Many British companies have names that sound foreign. The Australian and New Zealand Bank Limited is one example. Also, do not forget that investment in a foreign company can render one liable to paying a 'withholding tax' or a 'non-resident shareholder's tax', and such taxes can be as high as forty per cent. Expert professional advice should always be sought before investing abroad.

There remains to be considered the effect of your residence in Spain on your personal allowances and reliefs against British income tax. If you are saving British tax by virtue of some of your income being foreign, or treated as foreign, then you will not, of course, be entitled to full relief against British tax but only a proportion depending on the amounts of British income and foreign income.

Personal allowances have to be claimed for each British tax year. At first such claims will be made to your former Inspector of Taxes, but later, when your residence in Spain has been accepted as permanent, they will be made to the Claims Branch – Foreign Division, Magdalen House, Trinity Road, Bootle, Merseyside L69 9BB.

The Inspector will first calculate the income tax that would be payable on the whole of your income, whatever its source, as if you were still resident in the United Kingdom for tax purposes and were entitled to the full reliefs and allowances. The tax payable will then be reduced to the proportion that the income still liable to British tax bears to the total income. For example, if your total income in a tax year is £9,000, of which £7,000 arises in Britain and £2,000 abroad, as a resident of the United Kingdom you would be liable for tax of, say £2,000. When resident in Spain your tax liability will be reduced to seven-ninths of £2,000 – that is, £1,555.

Total income includes, of course, a wife's income and any tax credits in respect of dividends paid by United Kingdom companies. If the tax already paid or suffered exceeds the proportion of tax thus calculated as payable, the balance is refunded.

To qualify for proportionate personal allowances and reliefs, a person resident in Spain must be a British Subject a Citizen of the Irish Republic, be or have been employed in the service of the British Crown (or a widow of someone so employed), be employed in the service of a missionary society or have been previously resident in the United Kingdom and be now resident in Spain for the sake of health, or the health of a member of his family residing with him (Section 27 of the Income and Corporation Taxes Act 1970).

It is possible that as a resident in Spain you will become

liable to pay Spanish tax not only on any income arising in Spain but also on income arising in the United Kingdom which has not suffered British tax. In such a case you may be entitled to exemption or partial relief from United Kingdom income tax under the double Taxation Agreement now concluded with Spain. The object of such an agreement is to prevent a person's paying more tax than he would if his total income arose in only one country. More detailed information as to this can be found in the booklet on Double Taxation Relief (IR 6) obtainable from The Secretary, Board of Inland Revenue, the Inspector of Foreign Dividends or the office of any Inspector of Taxes.

You will see that there can be very considerable income tax advantages in emigrating to Spain, provided that you arrange your investments to your best advantage.

Apart from income tax, there is a further concession to those who live abroad. They will not be liable to pay Capital Gains Tax on any "gain" that arises on the disposal of assets after they leave the United Kingdom, provided that they eventually establish themselves as having been "not resident and not ordinarily resident" in the United Kingdom from the date of their departure.

B SPANISH TAX

In some respects the Spanish tax structure is similar to the British, but in others it is different. The fundamental liability to tax is the same. Anyone who lives in Spain for a total period of six months or more in the tax year will be liable to pay Spanish income tax that year on all his income whether it arises in Spain, Britain or any other country. But if he lives in Spain for less than six months, he will be liable to be taxed only on income arising in Spain.

The Spanish tax year is the same as the calendar year, running from 1st January to 31st December. Until recently a permanent resident was required to obtain a tax identification number, called 'a Fiscal Number', and also to make a Tax Return of his year's income by 30th April in the following year.

In practice few British residents of moderate means applied for a Fiscal Number or made a Tax Return. For them Spain was not so much a 'low tax country' as a 'no tax country'. However, when a foreign resident shows obvious signs of wealth – such as living in a large expensive house, owning two or more cars, employing full-time resident servants, having a private yacht or keeping horses – then sooner or later he is likely to receive a demand from the local Tax authorities, the *Delegación de Hacienda*, to complete a form disclosing his full financial circumstances so that a decision can be made as to whether he should be paying Spanish income tax.

Although the liability of making an annual Tax Return still remains, a British resident is no longer required to apply for a Fiscal Number. A new law, dated 1st February 1979, states that when a foreigner, whether resident or not, has to make a tax declaration, the number of his passport or residence permit will be accepted instead of a Fiscal Number.

So far the tax authorities have shown a lenient attitude to British residents, but this situation is not likely to continue indefinitely. In future one must take into account the possibility of having to pay some Spanish income tax, though the amount will almost certainly be considerably less than would be payable in Britain, and if you continue to be liable for British income tax, then it is unlikely that you will have to pay any Spanish tax at all.

The vital question, "How much Spanish income tax will I have to pay?", is not possible to answer with any precision at the present time. Today the tax structure is undergoing fundamental change following Spain's emergence as a democracy.

The new Spanish Constitution deals with taxation in Article 31. It states:

> Everyone will contribute towards the needs of public expenditure according to his means. There will be a just

> system of taxation based on the principles of equality and progress, but in no case will it amount to confiscation. Public expenditure will be reasonably adjusted in accordance with national resources, and the aim will be efficiency and economy.

One can, I think, take some encouragement from these words, and also from the fact that today Spanish taxes are only about half what they are in Britain. No doubt future Spanish Governments will increase some tax rates, but they will find it politically impossible to do this in a hurry. It will be many years, if ever, before taxes in Spain approach the burden of present-day British taxation.

Bearing this in mind, all one can do is to consider the position as it is today with a few simple practical examples, but first it is necessary to understand some of the peculiarities of the Spanish tax structure. The rates of tax vary according to the type of income. For example, the starting figure today for dividends is fifteen per cent, interest twenty-four per cent, royalties fourteen per cent, rents fifteen per cent and earned income twelve per cent.

As in Britain, there are a number of allowances and reliefs that can be deducted from gross income to arrive at the net taxable income. These include an allowance of 40,000 pesetas for married couples (provided total income does not exceed 1,600,000 pesetas – approximately £11,200), 25,000 pesetas, for each dependent child (50,000 if the child is physically or mentally handicapped), business expenses (if any), mortgage interest, life insurance premiums, donations to charity, alimony and special sickness expenses incurred in the year in question (British Chancellors should note this one).

When the income tax due has been calculated, there are further deductions for taxes already paid, called 'Schedular Taxes' (such as annual property and land taxes), also for any British tax paid or payable, and the tax due on the first 100,000 pesetas of earned income.

Now let us consider practical examples as to the tax position of British subjects who emigrate to Spain. For this purpose I use three imaginary married couples, Mr and Mrs Brown, Mr and Mrs James and Mr and Mrs Jones. For the sake of simplicity I assume that they are all in their fifties, without dependent children. They live on investment income, derived as to half from British Government Securities which are free of tax to those not resident in the United Kingdom (see Appendix II), and as to the other half from ordinary British stocks and shares.

Mr and Mrs Brown used to have a furniture-shop in a West Country town but decided to sell it and retire to Spain as Mrs Brown had for some time suffered from ill health. From the sale of the shop and their house they realized enough capital to provide an annual income of £4,000.

Mr James was a professional man in the Midlands who found that each year he was working harder and harder without any improvement in his standard of living, so the idea of early retirement to Spain became irresistible. The income from his invested capital came to £8,000 a year.

Mr Jones was a successful haulage-contractor. He was able to sell his business for a considerable sum and found that, when the proceeds were invested, like the others, half in Government Securities and half in stocks and shares, he had a gross income of £12,000. He had earned himself a life in the sun.

In real life of course the financial circumstances of our three imaginary couples would not be as simple. Some might have income from foreign investments, private pensions or Building Society shares, and pay life insurance premiums or have a dependent relative. All these would affect their tax liability, but the following examples show that almost anyone who emigrates to Spain will pay less tax. And that is true for the rich – and the not so rich.

MR AND MRS BROWN

Before the Budget of June 1979, the income tax and investment income surcharge payable on their income of £4,000 would have amounted to £1,070 as long as they lived in Britain. However, that Budget increased the allowances against tax, reduced the basic rate of tax and raised the threshold for investment income surcharge to £5,000. In consequence their tax liability while living in Britain was reduced to only £617.

On emigrating to Spain half their income becomes free of British tax, as it is derived from those Government Stocks that are tax free to residents of Spain. They become entitled to an allowance of £907 (half the normal marriage allowance) against their income from British Equities and are taxed at only fifteen per cent on the balance. The British tax payable therefore amounts to £164 (2,000 – 907 = 1,093 × 15% = 164).

However, as residents of Spain they become liable to pay Spanish tax on their whole income, and this tax might amount to £357, calculated as follows:

Total income of £4,000 converted into pesetas		572,000
Add annual value of their small Spanish flat		50,000
		622,000
Deduct reliefs of 40,000 for marriage and 50,000 for sickness expenses in the year		90,000
	Taxable income	532,000
Spanish income tax due–	200,000 @ 15%	30,000
	200,000 @ 16·02%	32,040
	132,000 @ 17·04%	22,492
		84,532
Deduct property tax paid on flat		10,000
		74,532
Less credit for British tax payable (£164 converted into pesetas)		23,452
	Net Spanish tax	51,080
	Sterling equivalent	£357

As a result of the June 1979 Budget and emigration to

Spain, the Browns' spending income has increased from £2,930 (£4,000 less £1,070) to £3,479 (£4,000 less £164 British and £357 Spanish tax).

MR AND MRS JAMES

This couple also benefits from the June 1979 Budget, but not as much as the Browns because they have to pay the investment income surcharge on £3,000. Living in Britain, they would be liable to pay £1,817 tax and £450 surcharge, a total of £2,267.

When resident in Spain, half their income becomes free of British tax. On the remainder they are taxed at fifteen per cent after a marriage allowance of £907. The British tax then payable amounts to £464 (4,000 − 907 = 3,093 × 15% = 464).

Like the Browns they become liable to Spanish tax on their whole income. In their case this might amount to £853.

Total income of £8,000 converted into pesetas		1,144,000
Add annual value of their large flat		100,000
		1,244,000
Deduct reliefs of 40,000 for marriage and 20,000 for charitable gifts		60,000
	Taxable income	1,184,000
Spanish income tax due–	200,000 @ 15%	30,000
	200,000 @ 16·02%	32,040
	200,000 @ 17·04%	34,080
	200,000 @ 18·06%	36,120
	200,000 @ 19·08%	38,160
	184,000 @ 20·61%	37,922
		208,322
Deduct property tax paid on flat		20,000
		188,322
Less credit for British tax payable (£464 converted into pesetas)		66,352
	Net Spanish tax	121,970
	Sterling equivalent	£853

In England this couple would have had spending income of £5,733 (£8,000 less £2,267). In Spain they have £6,683 (£8,000 less £464 British tax and £853 Spanish tax).

MR AND MRS JONES

The tax liability of our third imaginary couple when living in Britain amounts to £3,036 (£750 @ 25%, £9,250 @30% and £185 @ 40%), and in addition they have to pay an investment income surcharge of £1,050 (£7,000 @ 15%) which makes a total of £4,086.

When living in Spain, with half their income free of British tax and a marriage allowance of £907, their liability to British tax is reduced to £764 plus a surcharge of £150 – a total of £914.

The amount of Spanish income tax they might be liable to pay is £1,164.

Total income of £12,000 converted into pesetas		1,716,000
Add annual value of their luxury villa		200,000
		1,916,000
Deduct relief for charitable gifts of 100,000. There is no marriage allowance because gross income exceeds 1,600,000		100,000
	Taxable income	1,816,000
Spanish income tax due–	200,000 @ 15%	30,000
	200,000 @ 16·02%	32,040
	200,000 @ 17·04%	34,080
	200,000 @ 18·06%	36,120
	200,000 @ 19·08%	38,160
	400,000 @ 20·61%	82,440
	400,000 @ 22·65%	90,600
	16,000 @ 24·69%	3,950
		347,390
Deduct property tax paid on villa		50,000
		297,390

Less credit for British tax payable (£914 converted into pesetas)	130,702
Net Spanish tax	166,688
Sterling equivalent	£1,165

As with the other two couples, after paying £914 British tax and £1,165 Spanish tax, they have more money to spend in Spain than if they had stayed in Britain – £9,921 against £7,914.

You may be wondering why these couples when living in Spain are taxed at only fifteen per cent on their British dividends instead of the normal basic rate of thirty per cent. The answer is that today there is a Double Taxation Agreement between Britain and Spain.

Today, under the provisions of Section 497 of the Income and Corporation Taxes Act 1970, a British subject living in Spain, who can prove that he is liable to pay Spanish tax, is entitled to the following reliefs against British income tax:

1 Dividends received from British Companies will be taxed at only fifteen per cent.
2 Interest arising in the United Kingdom will be taxed at twelve per cent.
3 Royalties arising in the United Kingdom will suffer tax at ten per cent.
4 Annuities and pensions (payable in respect of past employment) will be entirely free of tax.

In certain circumstances other types of British income become liable to be taxed in Spain instead of in Britain, and in spite of the tax reductions in the June 1979 Budget, Spanish rates of income tax are little more than half the British rates.

The examples of these three imaginary couples are given to illustrate the differences between the British and Spanish tax systems, and to show how living in Spain can substantially reduce the tax burden. But everyone's financial circumstances are different, and tax laws are constantly changing. It

Las Palmas, Gran Canaria

Benidorm Beach, Costa Blanca

Holiday-makers at Palma de Mallorca

The port at Villacarlos, Menorca

The village of Nijar, Almeria

Salou beach, Tarragona

The village of Casares in the Province of Málaga, where Julius Caesar visited the spa

A typical patio in Córdoba

The village of Ojen, Province of Málaga

Toledo – the ancient capital of Spain

is therefore essential in every case to take professional advice to ensure that you get the maximum tax advantage from living in Spain.

If you emigrate to Spain to take up work, different factors will apply, but broadly speaking your tax bill will be less than for those living entirely on investment income. If your salary or wages are paid in Spain, the tax rate will be lower, and in addition you will be allowed the first hundred thousand pesetas free of any tax. Expenses necessarily incurred in carrying out your work can of course also be deducted.

Apart from Income Tax, Spain has other taxes in the same way as Britain. There are Value Added Taxes, Capital Gains Tax, Luxury Tax, Transfer Tax and Inheritance Taxes, but generally these are charged at lower rates than in Britain.

For the financial year 1978 Spain introduced for the first time a Wealth Tax. For those who live in Spain this is charged on all capital whether in Spain or outside. Capital includes properties, investments, personal chattels and cash deposits. There can be deducted from such capital all debts and charges thereon, and in addition an allowance of 4 million pesetas for a single person and 6 million pesetas for a married couple. A further 500,000 pesetas is allowed free of tax for each child under age.

A point to remember is that in the case of real property, i.e., houses, flats or land, the tax is charged on the 'official value' which is usually very much less than the market value. Luckily the present rates of Wealth Tax are extremely low. After all the necessary debts and allowances have been deducted, the balance of the capital is taxed at the rate of 0·2 per cent on the first 25 million pesetas (£175,000), 0·3 per cent on the next 25 million, and at increasing rates up to a maximum of two per cent on fortunes over 2,500 million pesetas (£17,500,000).

For example a married couple living in Spain owning a house worth £50,000 (but with an 'official value' of £20,000) and other capital amounting to £80,000 would at the present time pay Wealth Tax of only £116, as follows.

Total capital £100,000 (£20,000 + £80,000)	= 14,300,000	pesetas
Deduct marriage relief	6,000,000	
Taxable Capital	8,300,000	pesetas

Tax payable at 0·2 per cent on 8,300,000 is 16,600 pesetas, or £116. If they had a mortgage on their house, the tax would be even less.

Naturally these rates may very well be increased over the years, but for political considerations this is likely to be a gradual process.

People who normally live outside Spain and do not spend more than six months a year in Spain, are taxed only on their capital in Spain. On the other hand, they are not entitled to deduct the personal reliefs of 4 million pesetas for a single person and 6 million for a married couple. A British Subject living in the United Kingdom with a holiday house in Spain worth £50,000, but with an 'official value' of £20,000, would have to pay 0·2 per cent on £20,000, i.e., £40, which is not an unreasonable amount of tax.

When preparing your financial plans before emigrating to Spain, you must of course consider the matter of taxation. You will avoid paying some heavy British taxes but will probably have to pay some Spanish taxes. Almost certainly you will find yourself much better off and be able to enjoy a higher standard of living.

But always remember that tax laws, and the rates of taxes, are constantly changing, and no two persons have exactly the same financial circumstances, so professional advice at the time of emigration is essential. Most British banks have experts on international taxation and will advise how your tax bill can be reduced to the minimum.

Next to the sun and the wine, low taxation is surely one of the principal attractions of living in Spain.

CHAPTER 6

Preparing to Leave

Having decided that you want to live in Spain and chosen your new home, there are a number of important things to be done before you leave, and the first is to consider your financial arrangements.

A FINANCE

The careful preparation of a personal budget is essential. This will involve making a list of all your assets, including a cautious estimate of the proceeds of sale of your home and such furniture and personal effects as you will not be taking to Spain. Decisions will have to be made as to how this money should be invested and what existing investments need to be altered. For many it will be a matter of providing the maximum income and the greatest saving of British Income Tax, but it will be wise also to plan for some capital growth if possible. Discuss this with your stockbroker and accountant at an early stage. Arrange for the sale of any stocks and shares to take place after you emigrate and thereby save the payment of Capital Gains Tax. It is sufficient if they are sold only the day after you leave England. Your home can, however, be sold before you leave, as the proceeds are not subject to Capital Gains Tax. Other assets free of this tax are savings certificates, gilt-edged securities, private cars and personal chattels up to £2,000.

After preparing a list of assets, an estimated income and expenditure account must be made. This should cover the first three or four years of your life in Spain. Remember that during this early period you will not be saving much, if any, British Income Tax. Even the Government Securities set out in Appendix II will be subject to Income Tax until your status as "not resident and not ordinarily resident in the United Kingdom" has been finally established. This can take up to three years, though sometimes one is granted a provisional status as "not resident" much sooner. Each case is decided on its merits.

Remember also that during the first year or two in Spain you are likely to be landed with unexpected expenses "settling in". You may find that you need extra household equipment and different clothing or require a telephone. Time is needed to find the cheapest shops to buy food and clothing. It always pays to "shop around", and this is particularly true in Spain. When you are a resident you do not want to be paying "tourist prices".

In your budget allow plenty of margins and do not forget inflation. In Britain the recent Government has succeeded in reducing inflation these last few years, and it is hoped that the new Spanish Government will also be successful, but one cannot be certain. This is a problem that exists throughout Europe, and emigration to Spain does not solve it, though, for reasons I explain in other chapters, it is possible to live better on less income in Spain.

B INCOME TAX

At an early stage in your planning you must inform your Inspector of Taxes that you are emigrating to Spain. Read Chapter 5 on taxation, and if there is anything you do not understand, discuss it with him. By the time you have decided to emigrate, the law may have changed. In recent years British Chancellors of the Exchequer have become unduly addicted to presenting frequent Budgets. Your Inspector of Taxes will answer your particular problems and give you a form to complete so that you will be granted such reliefs and repayments as you will become entitled to by going to live abroad, and thereby becoming "not resident and not ordinarily resident" in the United Kingdom.

On this form, P85, you will be asked to state how long you, and, if married, your wife, have lived in the United Kingdom, the date of your departure to Spain and whether you intend to live there permanently. Particulars of all British income you will be receiving in Spain must be disclosed, and any accommodation retained in the United Kingdom by you or your wife. If either of you will be taking up employment in Spain full details will be required.

Any further information you may require about your tax position can be obtained from the Inland Revenue Claims Branch, Magdalen House, Trinity Road, Bootle, Merseyside, L69 9BB. However, if you have received salary or wages, or have a pension or allowance paid out of public funds in respect of Government Service, such as the Civil Service or HM Forces, you should refer to the Inland Revenue (Public Departments) Foreign Section, Ty-Glas, Llanishen, Cardiff, C54 5ZD, and quote your last Income Tax number if possible.

C EXCHANGE CONTROL

On the 24th October 1979 British Exchange Control was abolished entirely. Overnight – and for the first time in forty years – a future life in Spain became simpler and cheaper. Today we need only concern ourselves with Spanish Exchange Control, which is explained in Chapter 11.

This fundamental change in British law alters our former attitudes. For example, in the past it was an advantage to buy a Spanish property with Sterling and avoid having to pay the Investment Currency Premium, but now it is better to buy with pesetas. No Premium will be payable, and it will be easier to take out of Spain some, if not all, of the proceeds of a future sale. Remember this, as old habits die hard.

D BRITISH RETIREMENT PENSION

If you emigrate to Spain before you are sixty-five (or sixty in the case of a woman), you should make arrangements to continue paying your contributions so as to qualify for the British retirement pension. Up till now you will have been paying contributions under class 1 as an employed person or under class 2 as a self-employed person. When you live in Spain, you can pay under class 3 as a non-employed person. These class 3 contributions are entirely voluntary but must be made if you wish to receive the full pension.

ACT

The first thing to do is to obtain from your local office of the Department of Health and Social Security a leaflet, NI38, entitled *People Abroad*. The application form attached should be completed and sent to the Department of Health and Social Security, Overseas Group, Newcastle-upon-Tyne, NE98 1YX. Arrangements will then be made for your contributions to continue to be paid. The easiest method is for them to be paid in one yearly instalment by your British bank.

To qualify for the full pension, it is essential that total contributions should be equivalent to fifty weekly payments in every tax year for a period of ninety per cent of the tax years in a person's working life. A working life is normally taken to be from 6th April preceding the sixteenth birthday to 5th April preceding retirement age. It is possible therefore that contributions will not be required right up to one's sixty-fifth or sixtieth birthday, as the case may be. I had paid weekly contributions without a break from 5th July 1948 and continued when I came to Spain in 1971. I was delighted one day to receive a letter from Newcastle-upon-Tyne saying that I had already paid sufficient contributions to qualify for the standard pension and need pay no more while I remained in Spain.

Fully paid

A few years ago an emigrant to Spain was entitled to a British pension only at the rate in force when he became sixty-five (or when he emigrated if he was then over sixty-five), and he was not entitled to any subsequent increase. This was very hard on some of those who had retired many years before. Now, however, there is a Reciprocal Agreement between Britain and Spain, and a British pensioner living in Spain today receives exactly the same pension as he would if he were still living in Britain, and he is entitled to all increases.

E HEALTH

By emigrating to Spain you will be losing the benefits of the British National Health Service, but if you are in receipt of a British pension, either the retirement pension or a widow's pension, you become eligible to join the Spanish Health Service.

As you will not have contributed to this Service during your working life, a monthly payment will be required. As from 1st January 1979 this amounts to 1,982 pesetas a month for each independent United Kingdom pension. This is the amount payable by a widow, or a married couple who receive their pension by virtue of the husband's past contributions in the United Kingdom. If, however, a couple are both pensioners in their own right, because they have both paid United Kingdom contributions, they are treated as separate pensioners and each will have to pay 1,982 pesetas a month. They will then become entitled to the same rights as Spanish Nationals and receive free medical services and treatment in the State hospitals, which today exist in most Spanish towns. Even if they are not ill, they will save on the cost of pills and medicines bought from chemists. Today most modern drugs can be bought in Spain but are expensive.

State hospitals in Spain provide a good service, but they do not cover long-term, post-operative or geriatric care. For this you will need a private Spanish hospital. Their charges vary considerably, and to provide for this eventuality you should take out medical insurance. There are a number of private insurance schemes in Spain, but often the benefits are restricted to certain doctors and hospitals. It would be wise to join, or continue, one of the British insurance schemes which cover illness in Spain, such as the Private Patients Plan (PPP) or the

British United Provident Association (BUPA). The premiums vary according to the benefits chosen, the size of the family and the ages of the proposer and his wife. For extending the cover to Spain, or any other European country, premiums are usually increased by ten per cent.

A married couple without dependent children, who, for example, had joined BUPA some years before emigration and before the age of fifty, can provide for specialists' fees up to £150 and hospital fees of £225 a week (the average cost for Spanish private hospitals at the moment) for an annual premium of about £250. These benefits will, of course, also be available for illness when on holiday in Britain.

To join the Spanish Health Service, pensioners should obtain the United Kingdom Form UK/E17 from the Department of Health and Social Security, Overseas Group, Newcastle-upon-Tyne, NE98 1YX. The completed form should be taken to the nearest Spanish Social Security Office, the *Instituto Nacional de Previsión*.

Before you finally emigrate, you should, of course, arrange for a general check-up with your doctor and also be inoculated against typhoid and vaccinated. A visit to your dentist is also advisable. Unfortunately private insurance does not usually cover dental treatment, but most Spanish dentists are efficient and cheaper than in England.

Have your eyes checked and, if necessary, get new glasses before you leave, although in my experience Spanish oculists and opticians are well qualified, and their charges are very reasonable.

F IMPORTING FURNITURE AND HOUSEHOLD GOODS

Transporting furniture to Spain is expensive, and, apart from your specially treasured possessions, I think it is better to sell it or give it to your family and buy new furniture in Spain. Today there is an immense range of modern Spanish furniture in every town, well-made and generally much cheaper than in England, and it seems to look better in Spanish-style houses and apartments.

For those articles you wish to take with you, it pays to get a number of estimates from the many specialist removal firms that advertise in the British Press, as their charges vary considerably.

The permanent resident in Spain is allowed to import a large range of articles free of all import duty and taxes provided they are genuinely for personal use. These include furniture and furnishings, books, personal effects, musical instruments, works of art and bicycles – even motorcycles are allowed if their engine capacity is less than 50 c.c.

However, electrical and gas appliances for use in the home will be free of duty only if they have already been used. These cover such items as cookers, washing-machines, refrigerators, dryers, radios, television sets, record-players, vacuum-cleaners and floor-polishers. If you want new appliances, you are expected to buy them in Spain. Today there is a large range of all types, and buying them in Spain has the advantage of easy servicing, and spare parts are usually readily available. New television sets are, however, expensive, and it will probably pay you to import your used set and have it adapted to the Spanish system. Alternatively you can rent a television set in Spain. Today it is possible to rent a large set for black-and-white reception for only 1,200 pesetas a month, and there is no TV licence required. Most programmes are also transmitted in colour. You should take an electric kettle with you, as these seem to be unobtainable in Spain.

All the necessary paper-work involved in obtaining a licence to import free of duty and taxes will normally be handled by the removal firm or shipping-agent. Application has to be made to the Central Office of Customs in Madrid, El Dirección General de Aduanas, Guzmán el Bueno 112, Madrid – 3. A detailed list in duplicate will be required of all the goods together with a translation into Spanish. These lists must be signed by the owner and stamped by the Commercial Office of the Spanish Embassy, Flat 5, Hans Crescent, London SW1X 0LU.

Proof will be required that you intend to become a permanent resident in Spain. This can sometimes be a problem, as one cannot obtain a residence permit until one has been ninety days in Spain (see Chapter 7). You may be asked to pay a temporary deposit against any possible future liability for payment of duty and taxes, but this will be returned to you on production of evidence that you intend to get a residence permit. You can apply for a permit as soon as you arrive in Spain, and the police will give you a letter confirming that you have made an application, so that you can get any deposit back.

A declaration will also be required from you that none of the goods will be sold for two years after you enter Spain, and that you will inform the Spanish Customs of any change of address during that period. Permission to import household goods and possessions is granted only once, so that you will have to confirm that you have not previously lived permanently in Spain.

There is also a condition that the goods must be shipped within three months of the owner's arrival in Spain. This period can, however, be extended if there is unavoidable delay, such as a shipping strike.

If you buy your Spanish house or flat some time before you emigrate, then used furniture and household goods can be imported into Spain free of duty although you are not at that time applying for a residence permit. A written undertaking will, however, be required that the goods will remain for two years in the same dwelling and will be reserved for the exclusive use of the owner or his family. This undertaking requires the stamp of the Spanish Embassy or a Spanish Consulate General. The house or flat cannot be let to someone else, for this concession applies only to the applicant's second home. If you wish to let the property when you are not on holiday, you are expected to furnish it with articles bought in Spain.

Sometimes a non-resident is asked to provide a bank guarantee to meet the payment of duties and taxes that may arise during the period of two years after the goods are imported.

G IMPORTING OTHER GOODS

A tourist can bring in his British-registered car without any formalities or liability for duty and taxes. All that is required is the car's registration book and a document from the insurance company, called a "Green Card", confirming that it is properly insured against third party claims. It cannot be driven by a Spanish National (unless he is employed as a chauffeur) or by anyone who is a permanent resident in Spain, and cannot remain in Spain for longer than six calendar months. This period dates from the owner's entry into Spain.

In Chapter 9 I explain how a tourist can extend this initial free period of six months, but a permanent resident cannot do this. At the end of six months he must either import the car and pay the full duty and taxes, or take it out of Spain.

An application for an import licence must be made to the Spanish Customs Office, El Dirección General de Politica Arancelaria e Importación, Paseo de Castellana 14, Madrid, or the Provincial Office of the Ministry of Commerce. There must be proof that the car has been registered in your name for two years and that you are permanently resident in Spain. You will then be advised of the duties and taxes payable.

At the present time the import duties payable are on the following percentages of the car's value:

If it is older than 2 years	55·8%
If older than 3 years	51·2%
If older than 4 years	46·5%
If older than 5 years	41·9%
If older than 6 years	37·2%
If older than 7 years	32·6%
If older than 8 years	27·9%
More than 9 years	23·3%

The car's value is taken to be the CIF value of a similar car at the Spanish border – that is, the cost new plus insurance and freight charges. In addition there will be a luxury tax payable depending on engine size. At the present time this tax amounts to 17·6 per cent on cars up to 8 h.p., 22 per cent from 9 to 13 h.p. and 35 per cent over 13 h.p. In practice this means paying something like the car's market value at the date of importation. Why pay twice for the pleasure of driving a British car? It is far better to buy a car made in Spain, which will be easier and cheaper to have serviced and repaired.

If, however, you are emigrating to the Canary Islands, the car need only have been registered in your name for one year, and at the present time no import duty is payable. So if your future home is to be the island of Tenerife, you can look forward to driving your Rolls through the Orotava valley without this additional expense.

The same rules apply and similar duties and taxes are payable when importing yachts, motor-boats, pleasure-craft, motorcycles of more than 50 c.c. and caravans. In other words, they can remain in Spain for six months, but then they must be taken out or officially imported and the appropriate duties and taxes paid.

Unlike Britain, Spain allows domestic pets to be brought in by a permanent resident without any preliminary quarantine period. There are three documents which have to be produced at the Spanish frontier:

1 A health certificate in duplicate issued by a veterinary surgeon duly authorized by the Ministry of Agriculture.
2 An anti-rabies vaccination certificate in duplicate also issued by a duly authorized veterinary surgeon. This is not required for an animal under two months. Between the ages of two and three months it must have been vaccinated not less than one month previously, and if over three months old vaccination must have taken place not less than one month and not more than one year previously. If such a certificate is not produced, then your

pet may have to spend twenty days in quarantine and be vaccinated at your expense.

3 A certificate that the area in which the animal has been normally kept is free from animal diseases.

This certificate can be obtained from the Ministry of Agriculture, Fisheries and Food, Animal Health Division, Export Section, Hook Rise, Tolworth, Surbiton, Surrey.

All these certificates must be legalized by the Spanish Consulate General in London.

Finally, if you happen to be emigrating to Spain because you have just become the bride of a Spanish National, or of a British Subject – or any other nationality – who is permanently resident in Spain, you can import free of all duty and taxes your trousseau and wedding gifts. A British car is included provided it has been registered in the bride's name at least two years before the wedding. This gallant and benevolent provision of the Spanish law is strictly only granted when there is a Reciprocal Agreement between Spain and the bride's native country, and at the present time there is no such Agreement with Britain. In practice, however, the Customs authorities have a discretion, subject to certain formalities and investigations, to allow a British bride to bring into Spain her trousseau and wedding gifts free of duty and taxes. This is granted as a "concession" and not as a "right".

H CLOTHING

Unlike furniture, clothing in Spain tends to be more expensive than in Britain, and often of not such good quality. You should therefore start off with an adequate supply of British garments. Even in southern Spain warm clothing is necessary in winter. You may even be glad of an overcoat – but not very often. In the last seven winters I have worn mine perhaps a dozen times.

On the other hand, men's suits are of good quality and can be tailor-made for considerably less than in Britain, and being generally of lighter weight, they will be more suitable to the climate. There are a number of good dressmakers in Spain, and their charges are reasonable.

Spanish shoes and leather goods are world-renowned for their quality and value but are sometimes over-priced in the tourist areas.

I WIRELESS

To keep in touch with home affairs, a good short-wave wireless-set is essential and may be cheaper to buy in Britain. Buy it at least six months before you emigrate or you may be charged Customs duty on bringing it to Spain.

The Overseas Service of the BBC broadcasts regularly day and night and has world news no less than seventeen times every twenty-four hours. From time to time the wave-bands are changed, but they usually fall between the thirteen to fifty-one metre bands, or if you prefer it twenty-two to five megahertz. During 1979 ten bands cover Spain. In the morning the lower bands generally give the best reception, and in the afternoon and evening the higher bands. After dark it is often possible to get the British Home broadcasts on the medium-wave bands.

If you decide to live in southern Spain, do not make the mistake that I did and buy a set unable to get VHF – Gibraltar gives much better reception on VHF than on the medium wave-bands.

The illustrated magazine *BBC – London Calling* gives all the programmes of the Overseas Service and will be posted to you promptly every month if you apply to BBC World Service, PO Box 76, Bush House, London WC2B 4PH. The present annual subscription is £4 including postage.

J WILLS

Going to live in Spain is bound to change your life in many ways – exciting and delightful changes – but also fundamental ones. Your life style will be different, and also your financial arrangements. Therefore it makes sense to review the provisions of your Will, or if you have not made one you should do so before you emigrate.

When you emigrate to Spain with the intention to live there permanently you will probably acquire a Spanish domicile. A person's legal domicile is decided by the country in which he is living and at the same time intends to continue to live. It therefore consists of both a physical and a mental element. Apart from any specific declaration, a person's intention in this respect will be presumed from his surrounding circumstances.

The laws about Wills are different in Scotland from the rest of the United Kingdom, and if you live in Scotland you should consult a Scots lawyer. Anyone who lives in England or Wales however comes under the provisions of English law, which states that if a person dies domiciled abroad his English Will will only be effective to deal with his estate in England or Wales.

This means that a special grant of representation to a deceased's estate will have to be obtained in Spain before his Spanish possessions can be dealt with, and this is likely to be a long and expensive process.

The answer to this problem is to make two Wills, an English Will dealing with your possessions in England or Wales, and, as soon as you arrive in Spain, a Spanish Will dealing with your possessions in Spain. If you live in Scotland you should make a Scots Will and later a Spanish Will.

Therefore see your English or Scots lawyer, tell him that you are shortly going to make Spain your permanent home, and ask him to prepare you a Will to deal with all your possessions outside Spain. After you have emigrated, ask a Spanish lawyer to make you a Spanish Will dealing with your Spanish house or flat and other possessions in Spain. In this way much trouble and expense will be avoided for your family and friends.

In Spain there are various types of Will, but the normal one, called a *Testamento Abierto*, is what will be required by a British resident. It is drawn up by the local *notario* on the instructions of your Spanish lawyer. Many lawyers today understand English. Sometimes they can arrange for a Will to be prepared in two columns, Spanish on one side and English on the other. This is not essential but can be a help to your family and friends and save the expense of a translator later on.

A *Testamento Abierto* is signed and witnessed in the presence of a *notario*. The original document is kept by the *notario* in his registry, and he sends particulars to a central registry in Madrid, the *Registro Centro de Ultima Voluntad*. You get a copy endorsed with the official number under which the original is filed.

It is absolutely essential that both your English or Scots Will and your Spanish Will are drawn up by qualified lawyers. This is necessary to ensure not only that the Will is valid, in correct legal form and properly signed and witnessed but also that it is correctly worded so as to carry out your personal wishes. Such a simple statement as "I leave all my property and possessions equally to my children" can lead to doubts as to what you intended if one of your children should die before you. Do you wish the surviving children to take his share, or do you wish it to go to his wife or to his children? A Will prepared by a qualified lawyer will avoid such doubts.

A Will may appear a simple document, but much expert care and attention has gone into preparing it. It is a job for a specialist. No one would dream of having their appendix removed by anyone other than a surgeon. It is just as foolish and dangerous to try to make your own Will – or have it prepared by a friend who is not legally qualified.

And a word of warning about those Will Forms on sale in England. Do not touch them. It may save you a lawyer's fee at the time, but your family will almost certainly be involved in expense and delay in sorting out the problems that will arise later. I know, because I had to deal with such unfortunate cases when I practised as a solicitor.

An English or a Spanish Will can be changed at any time,

but remember that if you have acquired a Spanish domicile (as already explained) a new English Will, or a Codicil changing its provisions, will only be valid if signed when you are on holiday in England. Similarly a Scots Will should be signed in Scotland.

However, if you retain your original English or Scots domicile – because you intend one day to return to your native country – an English or Scots Will can safely be signed in Spain.

Emigrating to Spain does involve a considerable amount of preparation, and you should allow plenty of time to deal with the matters that I have mentioned in this chapter. In my case it took the best part of a year.

Finally, do not forget that under recent Spanish law you will now require a special visa to remain in Spain for more than ninety days, and this can be obtained only from the Spanish Embassy in London or a Spanish Consulate in the United Kingdom. It takes time for the visa to be granted, so apply at least three months before you leave.

CHAPTER 7

Residence Permits

If you live permanently in Spain, the normal thing is to apply for a residence permit – an *Autorización de Residencia* – and any foreigner who works in Spain for two years or more must have a permit. Such a permit is not only official permission to continue to live in Spain but also alters one's status from that of a tourist to a resident – and this has certain legal consequences.

Because of its beautiful climate and miles of golden beaches, Spain is the ideal country for a holiday. Tourism is Spain's invisible export and is very important to its economy. A tourist is therefore granted certain concessions which are not available to foreign residents or to Spanish Nationals.

Some of the concessions granted to tourists and not to residents are as follows:

1 A tourist can not only bring his British car into the country for six months without paying any duty or taxes or going through any formalities, but under certain conditions can continue to keep it for even longer. This is explained in Chapter 9.
2 He can drive his British car without a Spanish driving licence or Spanish insurance, provided he has a current International Driving Permit and a "Green Card" issued by his British Insurance Company to prove that he is covered against "third party" claims. As an alternative to an International Driving Permit, he can use a British

driving licence with an official translation into Spanish.
3 He can open certain types of bank accounts (see Chapter 11).

Because of these concessions – and other imagined advantages – many British subjects, and other foreigners who live in Spain, do not apply for a residence permit but continue in a state of "permanent tourism". Until recently the law permitted this practice provided certain conditions were fulfilled. After the first ninety days in Spain a tourist had to go home or apply for permission from the police to remain another ninety days. If such permission was granted, his passport would be stamped with a certificate of *Permanencia*, which, despite the name, is a temporary not a permanent authority to remain in Spain. It states that the holder of the passport is entitled to remain – "*para permanecer*" – in Spain for ninety days. At the end of this temporary period the tourist again had the choice of going home or applying for a second *Permanencia.*

Once a tourist had been granted two *Permanencias*, his holiday of nine months had to end. Two choices were open to him – to leave the country or to apply for a residence permit.

It was still possible, however, to continue to live in Spain without getting a residence permit by the simple process of crossing the nearest frontier and immediately returning to Spain, with one's passport stamped as having entered Spain. It was not even necessary to spend a night outside Spain. Many of those living in the south of Spain used to take a day trip to Tangier from Algeciras, or drive up to the Portuguese border, cross the frontier and immediately turn round and re-enter Spain. Then, by making two applications in due course for *Permanencias*, it was possible to remain in Spain for another nine months without having a residence permit.

I know many British people who have lived in Spain for years without having a residence permit. Every ninety days they leave Spain and immediately return, or by getting two

Permanencias they leave Spain every nine months.

Why do they go to all this trouble and expense? Because they imagine that there is some advantage in not having a residence permit. They think that they will avoid having to pay Spanish income tax, or that they will not need to apply for a Spanish driving licence, or that they will not be considered resident in Spain for the purpose of the Spanish Exchange Control laws.

They are entirely mistaken. Liability for paying Spanish income tax depends only on the source of the income and on physical residence in Spain. Anyone who has a permanent home in Spain, or who lives there for more than a year, must have a Spanish driving licence. Everyone is treated as a resident in Spain for Exchange Control purposes, unless he has a permanent home outside Spain and does not stay in Spain for more than six months a year. Having a residence permit is, therefore, nothing to do with liability to pay income tax or the need to have a Spanish driving licence, and from the point of view of Exchange Control it can have certain benefits.

The only real advantage in not having a residence permit is that it enables one to apply to keep a British car in Spain for more than six months a year, or, in certain circumstances, to continue driving it for more than six months.

However, the position has recently changed. The Spanish Government still wishes to encourage tourists and grants them certain concessions, but on the other hand they must be genuine tourists and not residents masquerading as tourists. So in 1978 new laws came into effect.

Those British subjects who come to Spain on holiday for not longer than ninety days – the genuine tourists – are not affected. All they require are their passports and, if bringing a car, an International Driving Permit and a "Green Card". Anyone coming for a longer period, however, must now first apply for a special visa. This application must be made to the Spanish Embassy in London or to a Spanish Consulate in the United Kingdom and should be made in good time as it can take several weeks before the visa is granted. It is also necessary to have the normal British passport valid for five or ten years.

Before the end of ninety days application must normally be made for a residence permit. However, if one's total period in Spain is not going to be more than two years, then one can apply for a *Permanencia* and remain as a tourist who has permission to stay longer than the normal ninety days. As such, the concessions for driving a British car will still be available.

The procedure for a tourist to obtain a *Permanencia* is quite simple. First you must register with your nearest British Consul in Spain and obtain a certificate of registration. This certificate, together with your passport and visa, must then be taken to a police station which has a department for foreigners, or to the office of the Civil Governor of the Province. A short application form has to be completed, and in a few days your passport will be ready, stamped with a certificate of *Permanencia* entitling you to remain in Spain for another ninety days.

A residence permit should be applied for a few weeks before the expiry of your first ninety days in Spain, or before your current *Permanencia* has expired. You will need, as well as your passport, visa and certificate of registration from the Consulate, four recent small photographs and a certificate from your local police that you are of good conduct. You take these to the foreigners' department of the police station, or in some cases to the office of the Civil Governor of the Province.

This time you will have to fill up a longer application form giving your full personal details and stating why you wish to live permanently in Spain. This form must then be countersigned by two Spanish nationals who are prepared to confirm that you are a suitable person to be allowed a residence permit. Finally you must produce some evidence that you have the financial means to support yourself. If you are taking up employment, this will be sufficient, provided that you are at the same time applying for a work permit. Otherwise a Spanish bank statement will normally be required showing that you have an adequate balance in your account or regularly import Sterling or other foreign currency. No minimum financial requirements are laid down. Each case is considered on its merits. If everything is satisfactory, the residence permit will be ready for collection in a week or two.

If you wish, a *gestor* will arrange all this for you on payment of a small fee. The permit lasts for two years and may be renewed for a further two years on evidence of financial means. Thereafter you can be granted a five-year permit.

These are some of the advantages of having a residence permit:

1 You are allowed to import free of all duty and taxes your furniture, household goods and possessions with a few exceptions, such as brand-new electrical goods which can be bought in Spain. Importing a British car is, however, a different matter, as has been explained in Chapter 6.
2 You, and your family, can each have a holiday allowance in Sterling or other currency (notes or travellers' cheques) up to 80,000 pesetas a trip, with a yearly maximum of 320,000. The allowance for business trips is 200,000 (max. 1,400,000 p.a.). Trips for reasons of health or study are limited only to the actual cost incurred.
3 You can apply to your bank for a loan to buy a house or flat.
4 If you are in receipt of a British retirement pension or a widow's pension, you can join the Spanish National Health Service on paying 1,982 pesetas a month for each independent pension.
5 You can apply for a work permit. Under the new laws the possession of a residence permit is essential if the work is to continue for more than two years. In some Provinces, however, it is the practice to insist on a resi-

dence permit even for short periods of work. Such residence permits are usually granted for only one year, the same period as the work permit.

These are all substantial reasons for having a residence permit, but what is perhaps even more important is that you are conforming to the spirit of the Spanish law. You have official permission to do what you are in fact doing – living permanently in Spain. If you should run into any sort of trouble, the fact that you have a residence permit will stand you in good stead.

It is still possible to avoid having a residence permit or a *Permanencia* by the tedious process of leaving Spain every ninety days, but I would strongly advise anyone who makes his permanent home in Spain to have a residence permit.

Your original status as a British subject entitled to a British passport is not affected in any way. It will make no difference to your liability to pay Spanish income tax or to the need to have a Spanish driving licence.

And finally, you have not committed yourself. If for any reason you wish to return to the status of a tourist, all you have to do is to surrender your residence permit by handing it to the police.

CHAPTER 8

Cost of Living

There was a time when one could live well in Spain on very little, and for that reason alone many chose it as the country for their retirement. Today that has changed, and it would be wrong to choose Spain as your future home solely on the grounds of cheapness. However, it is still possible to enjoy a good standard of living on a lower income than in Britain, or probably any other European country.

Until 1972 prices were fairly constant, and one could rely on getting at least 168 pesetas to the pound, sometimes more. Then in June 1972 the Pound was floated, and overnight everything became more expensive. I remember that a friend came on holiday that month. He bought pesetas at 171 to the pound, and when he returned home a fortnight later the rate had dropped to 152. Over the next two or three years the value of Sterling dropped even further, and at one moment the tourist rate was just under 100. Since then there have been two devaluations of the Peseta and the position has improved.

Over the last year or so the rate has fluctuated between 132 and 150. Throughout this book I have calculated prices at 143 pesetas to the pound. This is the average at the present time for residents who generally get a slightly better rate than the tourist by cashing their British Sterling cheques. This rate means that 100 pesetas are equivalent to 70 pence, 1,000 to £7 and a million to £7,000. Before 1972 the figures were 60 pence, £6 and £6,000 respectively, so the 'floating' of the Pound has increased the cost of living to British residents by about sixteen per cent over the last eight years.

On top of this we have had inflation in Spain, as in all other European countries. It came rather later to Spain than to Britain. According to the official Government figures it was twenty per cent in 1977 and seventeen per cent in 1978.

Some of my friends say that today it is as expensive to live in Spain as in Britain. I do not agree. We have not so far reached that stage, and I trust – and believe – that we never shall. I suspect that some of us who have lived here for many years do not fully appreciate how prices have risen back home. We are unconsciously comparing Spanish prices today with those prevailing in Britain before we left. The position is therefore not as bad as might appear at first sight.

There are some items that are more expensive in Spain, particularly if they are imported, but they are more than counterbalanced by others. Let us examine such basic matters as food, drink, clothing and housing.

The contents of a weekly shopping-basket will probably at first cost you a little more than in Britain. Meat, milk, sugar and tea are more expensive, but fish, vegetables and fruit are much cheaper. Alcoholic drinks, with the exception of imported Scotch whisky, are very much cheaper. Where else in the world could one buy a pleasant bottle of wine for only 28 pence, and a really good one for £2 or £3? A litre of gin can be had for under a pound, and a litre of Sherry or Montilla for under 60 pence. Note that I am talking of litres, not bottles.

When you have lived in Spain a little time, you will discover ways of saving on food. You will find that you tend to adjust to Spanish habits and eat less roast beef and steak, and more fish, fruit and vegetables – which are, after all, more appropriate to a hot climate. Pork and chicken are also good buys. Instead of buying groceries in the local supermarkets, it frequently pays to buy in a large town where prices are often substantially lower. To begin with, my wife found it useful in the village shops to stand close to a sensible-looking Spanish *señora*, see what she bought – and how much she paid – and then do the same.

A couple of years ago we joined one of the many hypermarkets that are now appearing in Spain. First I spent an hour with my calculator comparing prices over a large range of foods with those being charged in our local village, and found that they were between ten and twenty per cent cheaper. We pay 200 pesetas a month to be members, and this can be recovered in only one day's shopping. Luckily we have a deep-freeze and save time by shopping not more than once a week for essential needs. I very much doubt whether we now spend as much as we would have to in England. At the end of this chapter I give a list of some food prices in the spring of 1979, so that you can work out the cost of your own shopping-basket.

An important item in the family budget is that of clothing, which is certainly more expensive. This is particularly true of women's clothes, though my wife has made some excellent bargains at the sales. It is a great pity that Marks & Spencers do not exist in Spain. Men's lightweight suits, tailor-made, can, on the other hand, be quite reasonably priced.

It is in shoes and leather goods that Spain excels, in both quality and price – but beware of some tourist shops. Men's shoes should cost you about half what they would in England. My wife discovered a pair of most attractive Mexican-style boots for only £7.70. She was told by a London dress-designer that in Britain they would be about £40.

Houses are definitely cheaper, and I have already given some examples in Chapter 2. Rates and property taxes are also much less, often by as much as seventy-five per cent and great savings are made in heating. The oil-fired central-heating of my English home consumed 1,500 gallons a year. Here in our Spanish flat we keep ourselves warm in the short winter with a gas fire turned low most evenings, and very occasionally during the day. From November to March we usually need three cylinders of gas at a total cost of under £7.

Water is heated by electricity and our electricity bills for the year amount to some 20,000 pesetas (£140). Cooking by gas takes a cylinder a month and amounts to an annual expense of £25.

A large residence in the country will, of course, be more expensive. A friend of mine with a house having four bedrooms, four bathrooms and centrally heated by gas, found that last year she spent £300 on electricity and gas.

So much for food, clothing and housing. Let us consider other matters that figure in a family budget. Cars are cheaper to have serviced and repaired. Cigarettes can cost as little as 13 pence for twenty and small cigars 21 pence for a packet of five. There is no television licence required in Spain. Outside the tourist areas domestic servants can be found for well under a pound an hour, and it is still possible for two to have a good meal with local wine at a simple restaurant for £7 or less.

These items do not support the view that it is as expensive to live in Spain as in England, and there are other factors to be taken into consideration.

In any country the very fact of retirement brings with it some financial savings. You will be wearing more casual clothes. There will be no need to replace expensive suits for the office. Travelling daily to work and lunches-out will no longer be necessary.

Those who decide to live in Spain will need to spend even less because of the wonderful climate. The great expense of keeping your home warm in the long, cold British winters will be a thing of the past, so also will be the need for much heavy clothing. I find that I now wear an overcoat only one or two nights every year, and I should never have to replace it. In many unexpected ways there should be fewer calls on your pocket.

But perhaps the greatest financial benefit of all is the saving of British income tax when you live permanently in Spain. The examples I have given in Chapter 5 show this clearly.

I have often been asked the questions – "Can I afford to live in Spain?" and "How much does it cost to live in Spain today?" It is, of course, impossible to give a precise answer, even if one knows the full financial circumstances of the questioner. It is also necessary to know the standard of living required, and whether it is purely a material standard. On retirement many are prepared to accept some lowering of material standards in exchange for the other benefits. And allowance must always be made for inflation.

The answer that I always give to such queries is: "Whatever standard of life you are seeking, it will cost you very much less in Spain." There are three reasons for this. First, you will greatly reduce, or avoid altogether, the heavy burden of British taxation; secondly you will find that many of your needs cost less in Spain; and finally, you will say good-bye for ever to those constantly increasing fuel bills that are so necessary to survive a British winter.

When I first came to Spain, I estimated that a couple could live, simply but comfortably, on an income of about £1,500 a year. Because of inflation and lower exchange rates they would today need at least £3,000. They would be what I would call the 'back markers' and could afford to dine out only occasionally at cheap restaurants and with very infrequent trips back home. On the other hand they could probably afford to run a small car.

In conclusion I think it would be fair to say that, taking everything into consideration, it should be possible today to maintain a given standard of living in Spain on about half the gross income necessary in Britain.

SOME FOOD PRICES IN SOUTHERN SPAIN IN APRIL 1979

Groceries		*Pesetas*
Bread	300 grms	15
Butter (imported)	8 ozs	70
Margarine (best)	250 grms	36
Milk	1 Litre	45
Eggs	1 dozen	60

		Pesetas
Sugar	1 kilo	44
Coffee (instant)	200 grms	375
Tea	100 bags	200
Cheese (*manchego*)	100 grms	60
Bacon	100 grms	30
York Ham	200 grms	90
Luncheon Meat	100 grms	25
Meat and Poultry		
Fresh Fillet of Steak	1 kilo	540
Minced Steak	1 kilo	200
Chicken	1 kilo	135
Boiling Fowl	1 kilo	85
Pork Chops	1 kilo	300
Chicken Livers	¼ kilo	45
Fish		
Sole (small)	1 kilo	300
Hake (frozen)	1 kilo	135
Mackerel	1 kilo	66
Sardines	1 kilo	100
Fruit and Vegetables		
Tomatoes	1 kilo	16
Cauliflower (large)	each	40
Potatoes	1 kilo	20
Lemons	1 kilo	25
Oranges	1 kilo	15
Apples	1 kilo	28
Bananas	1 kilo	55
Onions	1 kilo	36
Cos Lettuce	each	15
Cabbage	1 kilo	30
Spinach	1 bunch	15
Strawberries	½ kilo	100

CHAPTER 9

Cars and Driving

In most parts of Spain there are good and cheap public services. Even small villages have their taxi-ranks and regular bus-services, while between larger cities there are modern fast trains and often air services as well. The trip between Málaga and Barcelona, for example, takes only an hour by a Boeing jet of Iberian Airways – a journey of more than 500 miles.

But Spain is a big country, and some of its most charming places are remote. To discover those little white villages sleeping high up in the *sierras*, and to visit friends who may live more than 50 miles away, a car is essential. Today the main roads have a good surface and are well signposted, and the last five years have seen a great increase in the number of motorways. Outside the tourist areas a car is also a help for everyday shopping.

When you live permanently in Spain, the most sensible thing is to buy a Spanish car. There is a wide range to choose from, either Fiats (in Spain called 'Seats'), Renaults, Fords, Citroëns or Simcas. Unfortunately British Leyland cars ceased to be manufactured here a few years ago.

Generally Spanish cars tend to be a little cheaper than in Britain. My last two cars – a Seat 124 and a Renault 5 – each cost about £200 less than similar models in England. Servicing is also less expensive. My last 5,000-mile inspection and oil-change came to £6.50, a new battery just over £30, and removing a dent and re-painting one side £35. On the other hand four-star petrol is expensive at 46 pesetas a litre (£1.46 a gallon).

A tourist can use a British car without any problems for a total of six months in each calendar year. If the car has been brought from a country outside Europe, such as the United States, Canada, Australia or New Zealand, this period is extended to eight months. It is important to remember that these periods are calculated from the time the owner arrives in Spain. If the car is brought in later, then it can stay only for the remainder of the owner's six or eight months. For this purpose the date of your entry into Spain should be recorded in your passport at the frontier.

This initial free period of six months can be extended by a tourist in two ways. If he is leaving Spain and wishes the car to remain, then he can arrange to have it sealed by the Customs for the remainder of the calendar year. From 1st January in the following year it can be unsealed and used for a further period of six months.

Alternatively it is possible for a tourist to continue to run his car for more than six months, provided he obtains permission from the Customs, and this will be granted only if he can satisfy them on the following matters:

1 The car must be permanently registered in its country of origin with normal number plates. A car purchased free of tax under the British Export Scheme will have tourist plates and will therefore not qualify.
2 Neither the owner nor his wife must be doing any sort of work in Spain.
3 During the previous year the owner must have imported, and paid into an internal peseta account, foreign currency equivalent to 600,000 pesetas (£4,200). If the owner is retired – a fact which must be confirmed by his British Consul – this financial requirement is reduced to 275,000 pesetas (£1,925).

Subject to these requirements a tourist can apply each year to run his car for more than six months, but after the first application a tax will be charged equal to ten per cent of the appropriate import duty, and permission will be refused after five applications.

A tourist, or a permanent resident in Spain, can, of course, import his British-registered car if he has owned it for two years or more, but the cost is so prohibitive that it is hardly ever worthwhile (see Chapter 6).

This initial six-month period applies to an emigrant as well as to a tourist, and it should be remembered that it is six months in every calendar year. A person who emigrates in July, for example, can use his British-registered car for the rest of that year, and until 30th June in the following year. By that date, however, the car must either be imported, and the full import duty and taxes paid, or be removed from Spain.

All these problems can be overcome by buying a Spanish-made car before 30th June in the first full calendar year that you are resident in Spain.

As the owner of a Spanish-registered car (a term which includes both a car made in Spain and an imported British car), you will have to pay two kinds of annual taxes. For cars of 8 h.p. or more there is an annual luxury tax, '*Tenencia y Disfrute*', and for all cars a tax similar to the British Vehicle Excise Duty called the '*Impuesto Municipal sobre Circulación de Vehiculos*'. In each case the amount of the tax increases with engine size.

Anyone who owns two or more cars will be charged the luxury tax on the combined horsepower of all the cars. For example, if you own two small cars of only 7 h.p. – which on their own would be entirely free of this tax, you will have to pay luxury tax as if you owned one car of 14 h.p.

The rates of these taxes in 1979 are as follows.

Tenencia y Disfrute

On the first 9 h.p.	–	100 pesetas for each h.p.
From 10 to 13 h.p.	–	150 pesetas for each h.p.
From 14 to 17 h.p.	–	200 pesetas for each h.p.
From 18 to 21 h.p.	–	400 pesetas for each h.p.

From 22 to 25 h.p.	– 700 pesetas for each h.p.
26 h.p. and above	– 1,000 pesetas for each h.p.

Impuesto Municipal sobre Circulación de Vehiculos

Under 8 h.p.	– 800 pesetas
8 to 12 h.p.	– 2,250 pesetas
13 to 16 h.p.	– 4,800 pesetas
Over 16 h.p.	– 6,000 pesetas

As with most annual taxes in Spain, there will be a surcharge if either of them is not paid on time.

The *Tenencia y Disfrute* is payable in the month of February on vehicles owned on 1st January. For the first three years from the car's original registration in Spain, whether a Spanish car or an imported foreign car, this tax is payable on the total nominal horsepower. During the second three years it is assessed on the horsepower less thirty per cent, during the third three years the assessable horsepower is reduced by sixty per cent and in the tenth year by ninety per cent. After ten years the car is exempt from this tax. In each case decimals are ignored when calculating the percentage deductions.

For example, the tax on a 15 h.p. car for the first three years would be 1,900 pesetas (900 + 600 + 400). In the next three years it would be assessed on 11 h.p. and amount to 1,200 pesetas (900 + 300). After six years it would be 600 pesetas on 6 h.p., and in the tenth year 200 pesetas on 2 h.p.

The *Impuesto Municipal sobre Circulación de Vehiculos* is payable every year without any deduction for the car's age. The month it is due varies from Province to Province.

These two taxes – and the high cost of petrol – mean that substantial savings can be made by choosing a small car with engine capacities of 1,000 c.c. or less, such as a Ford Fiesta, a Renault 5 or a Seat 127. But remember that if you own two cars, not only will the *Impuesto Municipal sobre Circulación de Vehiculos* be payable on each but the *Tenencia y Disfrute* will be charged as if you owned one car of their combined horsepower.

One 7 h.p. car will cost you only 800 pesetas a year at present rates, but two 7 h.p. cars will cost you 1,600 pesetas for the *Impuesto Municipal*, and a further 1,700 pesetas for *Tenencia y Disfrute* for the first three years – just as if you owned one car of 14 h.p. For this purpose a car owned by a wife is considered to be owned by her husband.

Next there is the matter of insurance. Unlike Britain, Spain has no free market in car insurance. The Spanish Government lays down minimum premiums to be charged for each type of risk covered. This prevents the cut-throat competition that some years ago led to the bankruptcy of several British insurance companies and car-owners suddenly finding themselves without insurance.

The law states that all cars must at least be insured against 'third party claims' up to a minimum amount of 300,000 pesetas (£2,100). This compulsory cover is called *Seguro Obligatorio*, and failure to have it is treated as a serious offence. The insurance certificate and the receipt for the current year's premium must always be kept in the car. At the present time the premium for Spanish *Seguro Obligatorio* for most cars is 1,535 pesetas (£10.73).

Over and above this minimum compulsory cover you can insure for all normal kinds of risk that result from the ownership and use of a private car. This extra insurance is called *Seguro Voluntario*, and the premiums charged depend, as in Britain, on the extent of the cover. First, you would be wise to have the cover against 'third-party claims' made unlimited, because such claims could easily exceed £2,100. The extra premium will only be about £10.

You can also insure against your car being stolen, or damaged by fire, and for repairs resulting from an accident. Some companies offer to pay the cost of reclaiming your losses against the driver of the other car, if he was the cause of the accident, and also the legal charges for your defence in any court proceedings. It is for you to decide how comprehensive you wish the insurance to be, and pay the appropriate premium.

It is usual for the car-owner to be responsible for the first £25 or £30 of any claim, and the premium can be reduced by having this amount increased. Also if you have no claims for the first two years, you will generally be entitled to a 'no claim' bonus of ten per cent for the third year, and twenty and thirty per cent for the fourth and fifth years respectively.

At the present time the total premium charged for full 'comprehensive' cover for a car of 950 c.c. is about £135 a year without a 'no claim' bonus, and about £95 with a thirty per cent 'no claim' bonus. However, as in Britain, Spanish motor premiums do increase every year.

When you buy your Spanish car, the dealer's *gestor* will arrange the insurance if you wish, as well as undertaking the other paper-work entailed.

Under Spanish law the following documents and accessories must always be carried on a private car:

1 A valid driving licence. This will be either an International Driving Permit, a British licence with a translation into Spanish or a Spanish driving licence, whichever is appropriate, as will be explained later.
2 A certificate of third-party insurance, together with a receipt showing that the current premium has been paid. In the case of a tourist driving a British car, this requirement will be met by producing the international insurance certificate, the 'Green Card', issued by your British insurance company.
3 The car's identity card, the *Cédula de Identificación Fiscal*, which shows the owner's name and address and should be visibly displayed. It is often hung from the interior driving-mirror. The registration book of a British car takes the place of this document.
4 In the case of a Spanish car its road licence, *Permiso de Circulación*.
5 Also in the case of a Spanish car a receipt showing that the current annual tax, the *Impuesto Municipal sobre Circulación de Vehiculos*, has been paid.

6 If you are driving someone else's car, a letter of authority from the owner should be available. Remember that, if you are a resident of Spain, you are not allowed to drive a car owned by a non-resident, though with your written permission a non-resident can drive yours.
7 A spare wheel and tyre with the necessary tools to change a wheel.
8 A set of spare light-bulbs and tools to replace a bulb.

In practice the Spanish police do not unduly worry a tourist, provided that he has his driving licence, passport and 'Green Card'. A resident can however be fined 'on the spot' for not carrying the necessary documents and accessaries. Strictly a resident should also carry his passport or residence permit, but the police usually accept a Spanish driving licence as means of identity.

The number of private cars on Spanish roads has increased considerably in recent years, and the chance of being involved in an accident is therefore greater. The Spanish are not normally dangerous drivers, but many of them are inexperienced. Some show little skill in positioning their cars correctly and tend to cut corners. When starting on hills, be prepared for their cars to run backwards, and never rely entirely on the indicator lights.

The great improvement in main roads makes driving safer, but during the long hot summers roads become covered with dust, and even a light rainfall makes them slippery.

The traffic police are vigilant, but I have always found them courteous and helpful. They are trained mechanics and, like an AA or RAC scout, will do their best to get you started again if your car breaks down. They have power to fine you for traffic offences, but if you pay immediately, you are entitled to a twenty per cent discount.

The driving laws in Spain are contained in a Code, the *Código de la Circulación*. It has 311 Articles and four Appendices and covers every aspect of driving. Many of its provisions are similar to those in Britain. For example, if you are involved in an accident or commit a serious traffic offence, the police can test the alcoholic content of your blood. If it exceeds 0·8 grammes per 1,000 cubic centimetres, you will be forbidden to drive and taken to court.

All cars must be fitted with belts in the front seats. In Spain there are no arguments as to whether one should wear them. Outside towns and villages failure to do so may land you with a fine of 1,000 pesetas.

Three of the main causes of accidents are excessive speed, driving too close to the vehicle in front and overtaking when it is not safe to do so. The Spanish Code deals with each of these in some detail.

Articles 17 and 18 of the Code make it an offence to drive too fast in specially dangerous circumstances, such as heavy traffic or reduced visibility. The fine is 500 pesetas if no other traffic offence is committed, but if the police consider that the speed is so excessive as to amount to careless or dangerous driving (*negligente o temerario*), then the fine can be as much as 2,000 pesetas, and in addition the driver's licence can be suspended for a period of up to three months.

Maximum speed-limits are laid down for different classes of roads. Since October 1976 these have been reduced in order to conserve fuel and at the present time are as follows.

1 On motorways, *autopistas*, and main roads 100 k.p.h. (62 m.p.h.)
2 On country roads 90 k.p.h. (56 m.p.h.)
3 In towns and at crossroads 60 k.p.h. (37 m.p.h.)
4 In places of special danger such lower speeds as are indicated on signs beside the road. These signs indicate the maximum permitted speed in red numbers inside a red circle. Speed signs in black numbers inside black circles are only for certain specified vehicles such as buses and lorries and do not apply to private cars.

Main roads, where 100 k.p.h. is permitted, are defined in the Code as those with verges at least 1·50 metres wide, or with not less than four lanes (two in either direction), or where there are additional lanes for slow vehicles.

On motorways and other roads outside towns private cars are permitted to exceed these maximum speeds by not more than 10 k.p.h. when overtaking other vehicles, provided those vehicles are not already travelling at the maximum speed.

The fine for exceeding the maximum speed varies from 250 pesetas if the excess is less than 10 k.p.h. to as much as 5,000 pesetas (£35) if the excess is more than 40 k.p.h. Today the police often do not stop you when you break these speed limits but use modern equipment which photographs the car and calculates the speed, and you do not receive a notice of your fine until later.

One of the most frequent causes of an accident is driving too close to the vehicle in front. Spanish law states that you must keep a 'prudent' distance behind such a vehicle and increase that distance in bad weather. What is a 'prudent' distance is a matter of opinion. A useful guide to this is based on your speed at the time. Take the first digit of your speed in k.p.h. and multiply it by itself. The resulting figure gives the safe distance in metres. For example, at 40 k.p.h. it is $4 \times 4 = 16$ metres; at 60 k.p.h. it is $6 \times 6 = 36$ metres; and at 90 k.p.h. it is $9 \times 9 = 81$ metres. These distances may at first seem a little excessive, particularly at the higher speeds, but remember that the car in front may have to pull up suddenly for reasons not apparent to you, and you will need plenty of room to avoid a collision. At 90 k.p.h. a car travels 25 metres every second, so a distance of 81 metres is used up in just over three seconds. If it has been raining, the road will be slippery, and these distances must be considerably increased.

Overtaking always needs the greatest care. The Spanish Driving Code lays down six specific cases when overtaking is forbidden.

1 When there is a roadside sign showing a red car beside a black car inside a red circle. Such a sign is cancelled by one with a diagonal black line between two black cars

in a black circle.

2 If it would mean crossing a continuous white or yellow line in the centre of the road. A dotted line on your side of the continuous line means that you can overtake if it is otherwise safe to do so.
3 Near a corner, a road junction or the top of a blind hill.
4 If there is another vehicle coming towards you less than 200 metres away.
5 If the car in front is likely to swing out to pass some obstacle or has indicated that it is going to overtake or turn left.
6 If a car behind you has already started to overtake your car.

Articles 30 and 98 of the Driving Code lay down three rules for overtaking. The whole exercise must be accomplished in a distance of not more than 200 metres; the two cars must not be parallel for more than fifteen seconds; and the overtaking car must be at least two clear lengths ahead of the other car before pulling in again.

When it is safe to overtake, the left indicator must be used in good time, and the right indicator used before pulling in again. Indicators are used to a much greater extent in Spain than in Britain.

The most common mistake is to overtake too slowly. When travelling at moderate speeds, it is essential to engage a lower gear so as to get the maximum acceleration and complete the manoeuvre as soon as possible. Extreme care is needed when overtaking very long vehicles one constantly sees in Spain today, and those with trailers.

For offending the Spanish laws on overtaking you can be fined from 1,000 to 5,000 pesetas, and in addition have your driving licence suspended.

Ignorance of the Spanish laws as to parking often leads to fines, and a distinction is made between parking and stopping for a brief moment. One may neither park nor stop in the following cases.

1 Close to a sharp corner or near to the brow of a hill where visibility is reduced.
2 Beside a traffic island or a building which has an entrance or exit for vehicles.
3 On a bridge or railway crossing.
4 In a tunnel or under a bridge.
5 In a place where it would obscure a traffic sign for other road-users.
6 At cross-roads or on a pedestrian crossing.
7 When there is a road sign prohibiting stopping (a red diagonal cross within a red circle) or where there are red and white squares painted on the pavement.

The difference between stopping or parking in these circumstances is that the fine for parking is usually double.

One is permitted to stop temporarily, but not park, within 5 metres of a road junction or cross-roads, within 7 metres of a bus-stop, and where there is a sign prohibiting parking only (a red diagonal line within a red circle).

And generally one must not stop or park anywhere if it would obstruct traffic or create a dangerous situation.

All these rules are really common sense and will be observed by experienced drivers, but in Spain one has to take special care with cyclists and pedestrians. Cyclists, including motor-cyclists, may be found proceeding the wrong way down one-way streets. The pedestrian often ignores the existence of other road-users – presumably on the principle that he was there first.

When you live permanently in Spain, you will need a Spanish driving licence. There are few aspects of Spanish law that cause so much confusion to the new arrival. First, I must make it clear that it has nothing to do with taking out a residence permit, or whether you drive a British or a Spanish car. Secondly, you cannot put off getting a Spanish licence by renewing an International Driving Permit every year, or by having a Spanish translation of your British licence.

Once again it is necessary to consult the Spanish Driving

Code. Article 261 of the *Código de la Circulación* states that anyone driving on a public road in Spain must have a valid driving licence, that he must always have it with him when driving and produce it to the police when asked.

The Article then sets out the various licences that are valid in Spain. They fall into five types.

1 The normal Spanish driving licence issued by the Traffic Authorities, the *Jefaturas Provinciales de Tráfico*. As in Britain they may be provisional or permanent.
2 Licences issued by the Military Authorities for drivers of army vehicles.
3 International Driving Permits which have been issued outside Spain by those countries, like Britain, which have ratified the International Convention of Paris of 1926 or of Geneva of 1949. They must be in the form prescribed by one or other of those Conventions.
4 National driving licences which have been issued by the driver's own country. They must conform in all essential respects with the provisions of the 1949 Geneva Convention and must be written in Spanish or be accompanied by an official translation into Spanish.
5 Any other form of licence which has been recognized by International Convention.

The British visitor to Spain, and the emigrant to Spain when he first arrives, must have, and carry with him, either a current International Driving Permit issued outside Spain or his national driving licence with an official translation into Spanish. A translation can be obtained at a Spanish Consulate in Britain, a British Consulate in Spain, or from the RACE (the *Real Automóvil Club de España*) in Madrid.

The British tourist is not concerned with any other form of driving licence, but a British resident in Spain must, within his first twelve months, obtain a Spanish driving licence. Article 261 of the Spanish Driving Code is quite specific on this point. It says that those licences mentioned in paragraphs 3 and 4 of the Article (International Driving Permits and national driving licences with Spanish translations) will be accepted only if the holder "does not have a permanent home in Spain nor has lived there for more than one year". Nothing could be clearer than that. Many British residents in Spain continue driving year after year without a Spanish driving licence in ignorance of this law, but ignorance is no excuse, and if they are caught, they can be in trouble.

Luckily, obtaining a Spanish driving licence today poses few problems for anyone holding a current British licence. In the past British residents were in the same position as Spanish Nationals. They had to pass a searching written examination on the provisions of the Spanish Driving Code and then a complicated driving test. When I came to Spain, the law had been eased. I was excused the written test and had to undergo only a simple medical examination and a very short driving test. In fact, all I did was to drive round the local football ground in a Spanish Mini with the driving inspector in the rear seat. It took five minutes.

Recently the law has been changed, and it is no longer necessary to undergo any driving test if you hold a current British driving licence. It is assumed that you can drive a car safely.

Like all other European countries, Spain has several different types of licences depending on the vehicle to be driven. The one for private cars (with a seating capacity of not more than eight passengers plus the driver) is a B Licence.

The minimum age for the first grant of a B Licence is eighteen, and the maximum is seventy-five – so do not put off your emigration to Spain for too long. Once you have obtained a licence, you can continue to drive up to any age so long as you are physically able to drive with safety. For those under forty-five a B licence lasts for ten years, between forty-five and seventy for five years, and over seventy it has to be renewed every year.

On a first application for a Spanish driving licence the following documents have to be produced.

1 A passport or residence permit.
2 A current British licence with an official Spanish translation.
3 A certificate of good conduct from your local police.
4 A certificate from the official Registry in Madrid, the *Registro de Penados*, that no court proceedings have been taken against you or are under consideration.
5 A medical certificate as to your fitness to drive, together with a photograph signed by the doctor.
6 Three further photographs, 35 × 25 cms, with your full names on the back and the number of your passport or residence permit.

A local *gestor* will arrange all this for you.

Anyone who suffers from a physical infirmity which prevents him from obtaining a normal driving licence can apply for a special licence under Article 267 (IV) of the Code. This licence will authorize him to drive a car which has been adapted to overcome his particular difficulty, such as hand-controls for the clutch or the foot-brake.

One result of these more lenient regulations is that your British driving licence will have to be surrendered to the Provincial Traffic Authorities and held by them so long as you live in Spain. For trips back home your *gestor* can obtain a Spanish International Driving Permit from the RACE in Madrid.

This surrender of a British licence will, I know, worry many British emigrants. It is a personal document like a passport, and one fears that it may get lost or expire. The answer is to have a photocopy made before applying for the Spanish licence and to make a note when the British licence expires so that an application for a renewal is made in time to the Drivers and Vehicles Licensing Centre, Swansea SA99 1AB. A lost licence will also be replaced free of charge and will be sent to the British address shown on your licence.

CHAPTER 10

Earning

Many who decide to live in Spain will have no desire to work. Indeed the whole object of the exercise is to escape from the "rat race" – the hurried breakfast to catch the 8.20, the long hours in an office, the crowded commuter-train home and finally the exhausted collapse in front of the television. One has been doing this for years, and life should hold more. The time has come to enjoy a fuller social life, to pursue some special hobby, to discover a new country and widen one's horizons – to grow younger.

But there are those who have different ideas. They want to continue to earn, to do something entirely new and, perhaps for the first time, to work for themselves. Others start with the idea of a complete retirement lazing in the sun but, after the initial honeymoon period, find that life begins to pall, and they look round for something to do.

It is never too late to start. Sir Winston Churchill and Grandma Moses never put paint to canvas until they were well into middle age. Few can hope to have their success, but it is very satisfying when the results of your efforts find a market, and a few extra pesetas are always welcome.

There are many opportunities for British residents to work in Spain, particularly in the tourist areas where English is required. Some act as hotel receptionists or assist property-developers. Some teach in the very many English-speaking schools or give language or music lessons in their homes. One couple I know run a very successful restaurant, and another a shop catering for the tourists who come out every year to their development. Others write articles for magazines for British and American readers, and for those who know Spanish there is a steady demand for translations. Painters, photographers and typists can often find a market for their skills. On the Costa del Sol the former Wimbledon Champion Lew Hoad runs a tennis school, a Scotsman manages a nursery garden, and to satisfy those who crave for pork-pies and English-style sausages, an enterprising pork-butcher has started a thriving business.

But there is need to strike a note of warning. Spain today has high unemployment, and the Spanish Government has to safeguard the interests of its nationals. As a general rule, no foreigner will be granted a work permit if there is a Spanish National available and qualified to do the work. One cannot rely, therefore, on being able to work at a particular job. A work permit may be refused. Most employment needs a work permit, and failure to have one is treated as a serious offence. Work permits have to be renewed annually, and the fact that you are granted one this year is no guarantee that it will be renewed. The local conditions may have changed.

However, a work permit is not always required in the field of self-employment. Such is the case where one is using special individual and artistic skills – for example, painting, writing, sculpture or music. Certain other occupations which are carried out in your home or done by hand, '*a mano o en su casa*', do not require a work permit. Among these are knitting, dressmaking, weaving, making costume jewellery and giving language lessons to a few pupils in your home. But if these activities develop into a successful 'cottage industry', such as giving English lessons to large classes or employing others in dressmaking, then a work permit will be required, and probably also a licence from the local town hall.

There is also the distinction between working for yourself and working for someone else. A pianist giving a single recital for a fee needs no permit, but if he is paid a salary for performing regularly at a night-club, then he must have one.

In the professions, such as Medicine, Law, Accountancy and Architecture, a permit will be required, and it will also be necessary for your British qualifications to be confirmed in Spain. This is known as '*convalidando el título*'. A British professional degree may avoid your having to study at a Spanish university, but a written examination will almost certainly be necessary. It will also be essential for you to join the appropriate professional college.

Applications for permits must be made to the Office of the Civil Governor of the Province, or if in Madrid, to the Gobierno Civil de Madrid, Paseo de las Delicias, 76, telephone 228.20.00. A permit is not now granted unless the applicant has a residence permit or a '*Permanencia*' (see Chapter 7). It is best for a new arrival in Spain to apply for a work permit at the same time as a residence permit (or a '*Permanencia*'' if his stay in Spain will not exceed two years).

The documents required will be the following.

1 A valid passport.
2 A visa issued by the Spanish Embassy or a Spanish Consulate in Britain.
3 A medical certificate issued by the Spanish Health Authorities.
4 Three passport-size photographs.
5 In the case of self-employment, a statement showing one's qualifications.
6 If employed by someone else or a company, the work contract in triplicate.
7 A certificate from the Spanish Ministry of Labour, *Ministerio de Trabajo*, that a Spanish National is not available for the job.

In some cases the application for a permit by a foreigner is published in the official gazette, the *Boletin Oficial*. This is to give a Spanish National the opportunity to apply for the job, which he must do within fifteen days.

If you have a work contract with a company, they will normally apply for your permit, but otherwise you must apply personally, and you will need the services of a *gestor* to deal with the paper-work. The ease of obtaining a permit varies considerably in different parts of Spain.

Some British residents have successfully gone into business, particularly those types of business which serve the needs of other English-speaking residents and tourists. Examples are bars or restaurants which specialize in British or American dishes, or libraries and newsagents with English books, magazines and newspapers. There are also night-clubs, gift-shops, dog-kennels, nursing-homes and secretarial offices.

In these cases you will require, in addition to a work permit, a licence from the appropriate Government Department or Town Hall. A new business will not be granted a licence if it will be likely to cause a nuisance in the neighbourhood or if there is already a sufficient number of similar businesses in that area. There are regulations, called the "*Reglamentos de Industrias Insalubres, Molestas y Nocivas*", which protect the general public and existing businesses and preserve the amenities of a town or village. They are the Spanish equivalent of the British Town and Country Planning laws. A licence is often granted to a new business on the condition that a certain number of Spanish Nationals will be employed.

The special laws applying to business premises depend on two things: whether it is a new or an established business, and whether the premises are bought or rented.

In the case of premises that are being purchased for a new business, it will first be necessary to have a contract drawn up by a Spanish lawyer. This will describe the premises, the purchase price and method of payment and the date on which the purchaser will get possession. If an existing business is being bought, then in addition the contract will need to state what fixtures and fittings are included in the sale and what sums are to be paid for the stock and goodwill. "Good will" is a valuable asset and is based on the probability that the present customers will continue to buy goods or services from the new owner. A business contract needs to be drawn with care, and later a formal deed of purchase will be prepared and signed before a *notario*.

If the premises are being rented to carry on an existing business, then the Law of Industrial Leases applies, the *Ley de Arrendamientos de Industria*. Under this law the business tenant has no absolute right to a renewal of the lease at the expiration of the current period. It is a matter of negotiation with the landlord, who can refuse to renew, or demand a higher rent and different conditions for the future.

Premises rented for the purpose of a new business however come under the Law of Urban Leases, the *Ley de Arrendamientos Urbanos*. In this case the business tenant has an absolute right to a renewal of the lease. The landlord can demand an increased rent in accordance with the official rise in the cost of living, but he cannot refuse a renewal, provided the tenant has paid the rent and kept the conditions of the original tenancy. A British tenant has the same rights as a Spanish tenant in this respect, because a Spanish tenant would have similar rights in Britain. In other words, the principle of "reciprocity" exists.

Under the Law of Urban Leases the tenant can sell the business and assign the premises to the purchaser provided he first informs the landlord of the price he is asking for the assignment of the lease. The landlord has the right to pay this price and regain possession of the premises. This is called the "*derecho de retracto*" – the "right of redemption". If the landlord does not wish to exercise this right, he must agree that the lease should be assigned to the new purchaser of the business. However, he then becomes entitled to a percentage of the price obtained for the assignment of the lease. If the premises first became business premises since 1942, this percentage is ten per cent, and for older premises it can be twenty to thirty per cent. The landlord has no right to a percentage of the price obtained for the sale of stock or "good will". That belongs to the business tenant.

Anyone thinking of starting a new business, or even of

taking over an existing one, should proceed with caution and take professional advice. Many British people have been very successful in running businesses in Spain, and you might be one of them.

But remember that, before you finally agree to buy a business or invest any money, you must first obtain a work permit and the necessary licences, and these will not be granted to anyone who has only the status of a tourist. Today it is essential to obtain a special visa and to apply for a residence permit, or at least a "*Permanencia*". Some Provinces will not accept a *Permanencia* and insist on a residence permit valid for one year.

The Spanish Embassy in London, or the Spanish Consulate General in Liverpool or Southampton, can advise as to whether a permit for a particular job is likely to be granted at the present time. General enquiries about working in Spain can also be made to the Ministerio de Trabajo, Departamento de Extranjeros, Agustin Bethancourt 4, Madrid, and information as to vacancies can be obtained from the official Spanish employment agency, Centro Nacional de Collocación, General Pardiñas 5, Madrid, or to the appropriate *Delegación Provincial de Trabajo*. In these cases letters should be written in Spanish and an international reply-coupon enclosed.

If, of course, you are lucky enough to be offered employment by one of the many British companies who already have offices in Spain, they will apply for the necessary permit and save you much time and trouble.

CHAPTER 11

Spanish Exchange Control

Like Britain in the past, Spain has found it necessary to impose certain restrictions to guard its foreign currency reserves and thus to limit the free convertibility of the Peseta into other currencies.

On the other hand foreign investment is most important to the Spanish economy, and to encourage this the Spanish Government has adopted liberal policies towards foreign investors. As a result, between 1959 and 1977 foreign capital invested in Spain reached the figure of 5,500 million dollars. In this way it is hoped to overcome Spain's two problems of a "balance of payments" deficit and a lack of sufficient domestic funds to reach the desired level of industrial development.

Spanish Exchange Control regulations are different for the foreign investor, the Spanish National and the foreign individual. We are not concerned here with their effect on Spanish Nationals or with business activities. Those British subjects who are interested in investing or trading in Spain should obtain from the Director General of Foreign Transactions two booklets, written in English. They are both called *A Guide to Business in Spain*. The first deals with foreign investments, and the second with Exchange Control and foreign trade. The address to write to is: The Director General, Ministerio de Comercio y Turísmo, (Dirección General de Transacciones Exteriores), Almagro 34, Madrid – 4.

As regards individuals who wish to live in Spain or buy private property, an important distinction is made as to whether they are resident or non-resident. This should not be confused with residence for other purposes, such as liability for income tax or the need to have a Spanish driving licence. It is also not just a simple question as to whether or not you have a residence permit. It depends on where you live – where you have your permanent home. Those who have both a British and a Spanish home are likely to be considered resident for Exchange Control purposes if they spend more than six months a year in Spain. The future British emigrant will usually be treated as a non-resident until he has finally moved to Spain and lived there for the normal tourist period of ninety days.

In Spain there is nothing similar to the former British Laws of Exchange Control or the Investment Currency Premium. Instead it is the funds themselves that are separated into different categories. Some are in certain circumstances freely convertible into other currencies, and others are not convertible at all or only to a limited extent. Spanish Exchange Control achieves its purpose by specifying the different bank accounts which may be operated by foreigners, depending on whether they are resident or non-resident in Spain.

For British subjects there are six main types of bank accounts, five of which may be held by non-residents and one by residents.

Each of these needs to be considered separately.

1 *Non-resident Accounts in Convertible Pesetas ('B') Accounts*

So long as you do not reside in Spain, you are free to open a 'B' account. It can be used to make any payments for goods and services in Spain, to make transfers to other 'B' or 'A' accounts, and also to purchase any foreign currency which is quoted on the Spanish Exchange market.

In the past these accounts have been highly prized for their convertibility, and British subjects living in Spain who formerly held such accounts were careful not to apply for residence permits – in the mistaken belief that they could continue to hold them as 'tourists', although they were in fact Spanish residents.

The present law, however, lays down that (apart from interest) these accounts can only be credited with convertible pesetas generated in Spain (that is, pesetas received from Spanish residents which have been expressly authorized as transferable by the Spanish Exchange Control Regulations), and transfers from other 'B' accounts. It is not possible today to feed a 'B' account by cashing a Sterling cheque, paying in a Sterling bank-note or making a transfer from an 'A' account.

2 *Non-resident Accounts for Payments in Spain ('A' Accounts)*

Again, so long as you do not reside in Spain, you are free to open an 'A' account. Unlike a 'B' account it can be credited with pesetas resulting from the sale of foreign currency, and therefore it can be used for cashing Sterling cheques or for receiving a transfer from a British bank account. It may also be credited with interest earned on the account or transfers from another 'A' or 'B' account, but not with Sterling bank notes.

This account is, however, not convertible into foreign currency and so can be used only for making payments in pesetas in Spain for any purpose, such as for goods or services, or for investment. It can also be used for transfers to another 'A' account, but never to a 'B' account.

The difference between these two accounts is therefore that, whereas Sterling, or any other foreign currency, can go into an 'A' account, it can only come out of a 'B' account. In each case it is a one-way traffic.

When the holder of an 'A' or 'B' account becomes resident in Spain, the account must be closed. The credit balance on an 'A' account will be transferred to a resident's ordinary domestic peseta account, and the credit balance on a 'B' account transferred either to an ordinary domestic account or converted into foreign currency and transferred to a foreign bank.

3 *Non-resident Accounts in Internal Pesetas*

These accounts cannot be credited with foreign currency, but only with pesetas that are not transferable abroad, and they can be held only by non-residents who have the permission of the Director General of Foreign Transactions.

They can be credited with wages, rents, dividends, interest, national lottery prizes and transfers from other non-resident accounts, but once such moneys are in the account they become 'internal' pesetas and can only be used for certain payments in Spain. These payments are for the purchase of property for the personal and exclusive use of the account-holder, for his personal expenses, for buying Spanish stocks and shares and for the credit of other 'internal' pesetas accounts.

When the holder becomes resident in Spain, this account must be closed and the balance transferred to an ordinary domestic peseta account.

4 *Non-resident Accounts in Foreign Currencies*

These accounts are generally used by foreign businessmen or companies for the deposit of foreign currency in its existing state without automatic conversion into pesetas. These funds may be converted into other currencies freely and, so long as they remain as foreign currency, are, of course, outside the normal Spanish Exchange Control system. If, however, the funds are converted into pesetas, they must immediately be paid into a non-resident 'A' account and then can only be used for payments in Spain and cannot be reconverted.

The ordinary British tourist is not normally concerned with such an account, and when he becomes a resident he is not allowed to have one.

5 *Tourist Peseta Accounts*

None of the non-resident accounts already mentioned can normally be used by a tourist for the purpose of changing his native currency into pesetas. The 'B' accounts and 'internal' peseta accounts cannot receive foreign currency at all, and the 'A' accounts only by means of foreign cheques or transfers from foreign banks. Without special permission from the Bank of England, a British tourist in the past could not cash his British cheques or arrange a transfer from his British bank.

The Tourist Peseta Account has therefore been expressly created for the needs of the tourist. Such an account can be freely opened and credited with Spanish or Sterling bank-notes, or travellers' cheques which you have obtained from your British bank or travel-agent.

This account can be used for all holiday expenses, and also for any expenses incurred in connection with a Spanish property, such as charges for electricity, water, telephone, rates, taxes and contributions to a community of owners.

Once Sterling has been paid into a tourist account, it is automatically converted into pesetas and cannot be reconverted into foreign currency. It must be remembered also that, on leaving Spain, a tourist cannot take out more than 20,000 pesetas in cash. Any amount over this will have to remain in the account until his next holiday.

These are the five types of current accounts that can be held by non-residents. All of them must always be in credit, and in the case of a tourist account the credit balance must not exceed 200,000 pesetas. Once you have emigrated to Spain, they will be closed, and you are limited to a current account in domestic pesetas. You may also, of course, invest in a savings account.

6 *Resident Accounts in Domestic Pesetas*

These are the normal current accounts for Spanish Nationals and foreigners resident in Spain. They may receive pesetas purchased with foreign currency, but they can only be used to buy foreign currency in the following cases.

a) A personal holiday allowance up to the equivalent of 80,000 pesetas a trip outside Spain.
b) An allowance up to the equivalent of 200,000 pesetas for a business trip outside Spain.
c) The cost of medical fees and hospital accommodation outside Spain.
d) The cost of students' education fees.
e) Assistance to close relatives who live outside Spain up to the equivalent of 10,000 pesetas a month.
f) In the case of British or other foreign residents, twenty-five per cent of any earnings may be remitted abroad, after deduction of any income tax or Social Security payments that are due.

The purchase of any further foreign currency requires the permission of the Director General of Foreign Transactions.

The number of different Spanish bank accounts may at first sight appear rather confusing, but they are an essential part of the Spanish system of Exchange Control. They are designed to conserve Spain's official reserves and at the same time encourage the foreign investor and help the tourist.

The United Kingdom resident who intends to live in Spain will normally be concerned with only two accounts, the Tourist Peseta Account until he emigrates, and thereafter the Resident account in Domestic Pesetas. If, however, he buys a Spanish property before he emigrates, he can open an 'A' account to meet the expenses of maintaining the property and receiving rents. He may also, with the Permission of the Director General of Foreign Transactions, have an 'internal' peseta account for purely peseta transactions, until he becomes a resident in Spain.

Finally, it remains to be considered how the Spanish laws of Exchange Control affect those who sell their Spanish properties while still resident in the United Kingdom.

Always provided that the property was originally purchased by a 'foreign money contribution' (i.e. the necessary pesetas were purchased with Sterling), you can take out of Spain the following amounts:

1 Rents received, if the full purchase price has been paid and all tax liabilities met.
2 The proceeds of sale subject to certain conditions. These are: a) that you can prove that it was originally bought with a 'foreign money contribution', which has been recorded in the Property Register and the Foreign Investment Register; b) that at the time of the sale you are not resident in Spain; c) that if the purchaser is not resident in Spain the price is paid by a 'foreign money contribution'; and d) that the price received is not, in the opinion of the Director General of Foreign Transactions, a 'speculative activity'.

However, a word of warning is necessary. The 'official value' recorded in the *Escritura* is usually considerably less than the actual price paid. If your 'foreign money contribution' has been recorded at this value in the Foreign Investment Register, you will be able to take out only this amount plus a reasonable profit.

You can sell to another British resident for Sterling, and when he comes to sell he will have the benefit of your original 'foreign money contribution', provided it has been duly recorded. If however you withdraw your 'contribution' and take only the balance in Sterling, the new purchaser will lose this benefit.

If you sell when still resident in Spain to another Spanish resident, you have no right to transfer any of the proceeds of sale to the United Kingdom, but of course they can be used to buy another Spanish property.

When, however, you eventually return to the United Kingdom and cease to be a resident of Spain, you can apply to the Director General of Foreign transactions through your

Spanish Bank to have an 'Internal Peseta Account'. Any proceeds of sale of your former Spanish property that are blocked in Spain can then be paid into this account. Out of the moneys in this account you can invest in shares of a company officially quoted on the Spanish Stock Exchange or in Spanish Government bonds or fixed interest securities. After this investment has remained unchanged for three years, it can be sold and the proceeds remitted to the United Kingdom. During the three years all interest, dividends and the proceeds of subscription rights can be paid into your British bank.

In addition, anyone who returns to his native country for reasons of health can apply to the Director General of Foreign Transactions for permission to take out of Spain money in excess of the normal amounts.

These are the main provisions of Spanish Exchange Control at the present moment that are likely to affect British subjects, but these regulations are changed from time to time. Before making any financial transaction you should always take advice from a Spanish lawyer or your Spanish bank manager.

CHAPTER 12

The American in Spain

The other day I was talking to a friend in an American Consulate and mentioned that I was writing a book on living in Spain. His immediate response was that it would be of considerable interest to the many Americans who have made their homes in Spain or were thinking of doing so. That decided me to include a chapter especially for American readers.

Most of what I have written about life in modern Spain applies to American as well as British residents, and so also, with just two minor exceptions, do the laws of Spain. It is the former British laws about Exchange Control and taxation that are not relevant, and so I will start with these subjects.

American Exchange Control is soon dealt with, because it does not exist. American Citizens can buy Spanish houses, flats or land without any permission from their Government and can change dollars into pesetas whenever they wish. They do not have to pay an Investment Currency Premium or apply for an emigration allowance. All that American law requires is that a record is kept of amounts over 5,000 dollars which are converted into pesetas. The reason for this one simple condition is that it provides a check on international fraud.

American residents in Spain start off in the same position as British residents now do (since the 24th October 1979). Both are free from Exchange Control restrictions imposed by their native countries, but both are, of course, equally subject to the Spanish laws on Exchange Control, which are explained in the previous chapter.

Like the British, Americans will enjoy considerable tax advantages from living in Spain, but how much tax will be saved depends on their personal circumstances and the American tax laws. I am not qualified to advise on this, but I am told that, whereas all American citizens remain liable to pay federal taxes when they live in Spain – or in any other foreign country – great savings can be made in state taxes. In every case professional advice should be obtained from an American accountant or lawyer.

The Spanish laws on such matters as buying, selling and letting properties, owning and driving cars, paying taxes, working and residence permits are the same for all foreign residents, American, British or any other nationality. However, there are two concessions granted to those who come to Spain from a country outside Europe, such as the United States, Australia and New Zealand. These concessions affect the laws as to residence permits and using foreign-registered cars.

The new arrival from the United States can stay in Spain without the need to apply for a *Permanencia* or a residence permit for an initial period of 180 days – twice as long as those who have come from the United Kingdom. At the end of this period an American must either leave Spain or apply for a *Permanencia* or a residence permit. However, he will be allowed only one *Permanencia* lasting for ninety days, unlike Europeans who can apply for two *Permanencias*. After his one *Permanencia*, he must apply for a residence permit or leave Spain.

The American tourist with his 180 days free period plus a *Permanencia* lasting ninety days can extend his Spanish holiday for a total of nine months, just the same time as a British tourist with his ninety days free period and two *Permanencias* of ninety days each.

However, an American who wishes to be granted a *Permanencia* or residence permit should obtain a special visa from a Spanish Consulate in America. Failure to produce such a visa could result in his application being refused. At the moment in some Provinces a visa is not always asked for, but it is likely that it will be in the future.

The other concession granted to Americans concerns American-registered cars. Such cars can be freely used without any restrictions for eight months in any calendar year. This period dates from the owner's arrival in Spain, so it is important to have one's passport stamped at the Spanish frontier. As I have already explained in Chapter 9, this free period is calculated on the calendar year. An American who brings his car to Spain after 30th April can continue to drive his car free of restriction until 31st August in the following year.

At the end of this free period an American car can be kept in Spain only if it is officially imported and the appropriate duties and taxes paid, if it is sealed by the Spanish Customs for the remainder of the year or if special permission is obtained to continue to run it. The three conditions that must be satisfied for such permission are set out in Chapter 9. One of these is that the car has permanent registration in its country of origin, and this could cause a problem in those American states where cars are registered for only one year.

Apart from these minor differences, the information given in this book applies to American citizens in the same manner as to British subjects. American readers may, however, like to have a list of some schools that teach according to the American educational system, and also the addresses and telephone numbers of the United States Embassy and the principal American Consulates and Consular Agencies in Spain and the Spanish Islands.

AMERICAN SCHOOLS

Madrid	The American School of Madrid, Apartado 80, Madrid.
Barcelona	The American School of Barcelona, Plaza Eusebio Guell 8, Barcelona-17.

	The American International School of Barcelona, Teodoro Roviralta 33, Barcelona-6.
	The Anglo-American School, Paseo de Barbi 152, Castelldefels, Barcelona.
Bilbao	The American School of Bilbao, Apartado 38, Las Arenas, Vicaya.
	The Anglo-American School, Valdes 14, Las Arenas, Viscaya.
The Balearics	The American School of Mallorca, La Casona, Calle Oratorio, Portals Nous, Calvia, Mallorca.
	The Baleares International School, Cami Son Toells y Calle Cabo Mateu Coch, San Austin, Mallorca.
	The Ibiza International School, Apartado 438, Ibiza.
The Canary Islands	The American School of Las Palmas, Carretera de los Hoyos Km. 5, Marzagan, Las Palmas, Gran Canaria.

Note: Many of the British schools listed in Appendix VII also prepare pupils for entry into American schools and universities.

THE AMERICAN EMBASSY AND CONSULATES

The Embassy of the United States of America, Serrano 75, Madrid.
Tel. (91) 276.34.00

Barcelona	Consulate-General, Via Layetana 33/34, Barcelona. Tel. (93) 319.95.50
Bilbao	Consulate, Avenida del Ejercito 11, Bilbao-4. Tel. (94) 435.83.00

Madrid	Consulate-General, Serrano 75, Madrid-6. Tel. (91) 276.34.00
Seville	Consulate-General, Paseo de las Delicias 7, Seville. Tel. (954) 23.18.85

AMERICAN CONSULAR AGENCIES

The Balearics	Avenida Jaime 111 26, Palma de Mallorca, Mallorca. Tel. (971) 22.26.60
The Canary Islands	General Primo de Rivera 5, Las Palmas, Gran Canaria. Tel. (928) 27.12.59
Málaga	Ramon y Cajal, Edificio el Ancla, Fuengirola, (Málaga). Tel. (952) 46.18.65
Valencia	Ribera 3, Valencia. Tel. (988) 321.69.73

CHAPTER 13

Family Law and Nationality

The importance of making a Will – or better two Wills – has already been mentioned in Chapter 6, but there are other family matters that are likely to concern some emigrants to Spain.

It has not been unknown for British and American residents to fall in love and decide to marry someone of their own nationality or of Spanish or other nationality. They may need to register a birth or a death, or decide to take up Spanish nationality. It is therefore necessary to consider what Spanish law says about these important subjects.

They are all matters which should be discussed with your consulate, because consuls and their officers are specially trained to deal with the problems that may arise and are always willing to help.

Let us consider therefore births, marriages and deaths.

BIRTHS

Registration of all births in Spain is compulsory, and this is so whatever the nationality of the parents and whether they live permanently in Spain or are there for only a temporary period.

Either parent, or the midwife present at the birth, must within eight days register the birth at the Civil Registry which is usually located in the Town Hall. A declaration has to be made stating the child's full names and surname, the names of both parents, the hour, date and place of birth, and finally whether or not it is legitimate. Under Article 108 of the Spanish Civil Code a child is deemed legitimate if it is born 180 days or more after the date of its parents' marriage or within three hundred days of the annulment of the marriage. In addition to this declaration, a certificate, signed by a doctor or matron on an official form, will be required.

Spanish birth certificates are issued in two forms. There is a short one, called an '*extracto*' or a '*certificado simple*' which gives only the child's names, the parents' names and the date of birth. A foreign parent should always ask for the longer form, called the '*certificado literal de nacimiento*', which gives full details of the registration.

Next the birth should be registered at the parents' consulate. The documents that will be required are the Spanish birth certificate, the father's passport and the parents' birth certificates and marriage certificate. The child of a British father will be entitled to be issued with a British birth certificate, and the birth will in due course be registered with the Registrar General, St Catherine's House, London.

Registration at a British consulate should be made without undue delay. In the case of a child of a father who was born in Britain registration can in fact take place at any time, but it must otherwise be made within one year of the birth.

The children of foreign parents can be baptized into the Roman Catholic Faith at any Spanish church, or into the Protestant Faith at one of the many Anglican churches in Spain.

MARRIAGES

Being a Roman Catholic country, Spain considers that a marriage is both a religious and a civil matter. The union has to be solemnized and blessed in church and legalized and registered by the State. At the present time there is no divorce in Spain, but it is, of course, possible for a Spanish marriage to be dissolved under the laws of other countries. However, such foreign divorce decrees will not be recognized in Spain. Under Spanish law the parties are still married.

The April Fair at Seville

The *fiesta* of 'Pero Palo' at Villanueva de la Vera in the Province of Cáceres

Harvest-time in Penedés

A sherry *solera*

Cadaqués in the Province of Gerona

The fourteenth-century Gothic cathedral of Palma de Mallorca

La Mesquita – the great mosque at Córdoba, which once rivalled Mecca as a place of pilgrimage for the Moslem

The eastern façade of the mosque at Córdoba

The Cathedral of the Holy Family, Barcelona

The Church of Santa Maria, Arcos de la Frontera

The Gothic cathedral, Toledo – the seat of the Primate of Spain

The Cathedral of the Holy Family, Barcelona

The Church of Santa Maria, Arcos de la Frontera

The Gothic cathedral, Toledo – the seat of the Primate of Spain

The fishing-port of Cadaqués, Costa Brava

Folding the nets – Lequeitio, Viscaya

The 'Romería del Rocio' – the famous pilgrimage to the shrine of Our Lady of Rocio, 'the White Dove'

It is possible that at some time in the future divorce will be recognized in Spain, because Article 32 of the new Spanish Constitution specifically mentions the word 'dissolution'. This will, however, have to be a matter for special legislation.

When both parties are Roman Catholics, marriage is simple. First they attend before a judge of the Civil Registry and prove that they are both single and of age. Then they go to the parish priest, who arranges the wedding in the local church. The religious ceremony is attended by the judge or his deputy, and finally the marriage certificate is issued.

If only one of the parties is a Roman Catholic, it is still possible for them to be married in church, but special permission will have to be obtained from a higher authority than the parish priest, and the ceremony may have to take place in a chapel rather than a church. In the past the non-Catholic party had to agree that any children of the marriage would be baptized in to the Roman Catholic Faith, but this undertaking is no longer required.

When neither of the parties is Roman Catholic, they cannot be married in a Spanish church. Anglican churches in Spain are forbidden to conduct marriage ceremonies. If the couple want a church wedding, they must return to their native country. However, they can still have a civil ceremony before a judge.

Each of them will be required to make a statement under oath that they are not Roman Catholic and prove that they are single and have lived in Spain for at least two years. Passports and birth certificates must be produced, and a widow or widower will need a death certificate of their former spouse and possibly also a certificate of the former marriage.

A divorced person can have a registry marriage in Spain provided two conditions are satisfied: the former marriage must have been purely a civil ceremony and not solemnized in a church, and there must be a valid Decree of Divorce. Generally a special certificate, a '*certificado de ley*', will also be required to prove that the divorce was valid according to the laws of the country where it was obtained. This certificate is drawn up and signed by a qualified lawyer of that country.

As an alternative to a Spanish civil marriage, British subjects can be married at certain British consulates in Spain, but in practice they are usually advised to be married in Gibraltar, particularly if they live in southern Spain. Under the Marriage Ordinance of Gibraltar a British subject or an American citizen can be married under a Special Licence granted by the Governor of Gibraltar, and there is no need to establish any residential qualification.

To obtain such a licence the following documents are needed:

1 An affidavit made by one of the parties to the intended marriage. The necessary form can be obtained at a British or American consulate. It sets out the full names and addresses of both parties and their dates of birth and has to be signed and sworn before either a British Commissioner for Oaths or a British Consular Officer.
2 If either of the parties is under age, the written consent of the parent or guardian will be required. A British subject comes of age at eighteen and an American citizen at eighteen or twenty-one, depending on which of the American States was the place of his or her birth.
3 A divorced person will need to produce the original or certified copy of the Decree Absolute or Final Decree of Divorce, and, if it was issued outside Britain or Gibraltar, it will generally need to be legally authenticated by the British Consular Authority for the place where it was granted.
4 A widow or a widower must produce the death certificate of the former spouse, and if this does not disclose his or her relationship to the deceased, the marriage certificate will also be required.

The affidavit and necessary documents should be sent by post, together with a bank draft for the fees, to the Registrar of Marriages, 30b Town Range, Gibraltar. If everything is in order, the Governor's Special Licence will be issued in a few days and an appointment made for the parties to attend the Registry. They should take their passports with them and arrange for two witnesses. The ceremony will be conducted in English. The minimum age for a Gibraltarian marriage is fourteen for a girl and sixteen for a boy.

DEATHS

Deaths must be registered at the local Civil Registry by a relative or friend, who should have a doctor's certificate stating the cause of death. The Spanish death certificate is then taken to the deceased's appropriate consulate which will issue their certificate.

In most large Spanish towns today there are cemeteries for the burial of non-Roman Catholics, so that should not cause any problem. If the next-of-kin wishes, the body can be flown back to the United Kingdom, but this is an expensive procedure.

A deceased's assets in Spain cannot be dealt with until the appropriate inheritance taxes have been calculated and paid. A Spanish lawyer should therefore be instructed without delay. First he will send a copy of the death certificate to the Central Registry in Madrid and request a '*certificado de ultima voluntad*', a certificate of the last wishes of the deceased. This certificate states whether a Will has been made, and, if so, the date that it was signed and the *notario*'s office where the original is deposited. Next the lawyer sends a certified copy of the Will together with a complete list of the deceased's Spanish assets to the office which assesses the amount of inheritance taxes payable. This must be done within six months of death or there will be a surcharge of ten per cent, or even more if there is undue delay.

If the deceased has not made a valid Will, then his assets go to his next-of-kin according to the laws of his native country, unless he has become a Spanish National.

NATIONALITY

A person's nationality is an important aspect of his or her life and carries with it both rights and obligations. You have the right to live and work in the country of which you are a national, and the right to the protection of that country even when you live elsewhere. On the other hand, the laws of your country lay down certain obligations, such as the need to support your family and to provide for them in your Will. If you do not make a Will, such laws determine who will inherit your possessions.

To start with, you have a nationality by birth, which is usually determined by the nationality of your father, or in some cases of your mother or the place of birth. This is nationality by chance. Later you can acquire a new nationality – a nationality by choice – and thereby gain new rights and undertake new obligations. In certain circumstances it is possible to have dual nationality, though the laws of most countries attempt to prevent this happening.

Emigration to Spain by itself has no effect on your nationality, nor does the decision to apply for a Spanish residence permit nor the fact that you have no intention of returning to your native country. If, and until, you acquire a new nationality by choice, you remain a British or an American National with all the rights and obligations that this involves.

Nationality starts at birth, so let us consider the position of a child born in Spain. If the father is British, the child will have British nationality, provided the birth is registered at a British consulate. However, if the father is Spanish and the mother British, the child will have Spanish nationality only, because at the present time the nationality of a British mother is not transmitted to her child if it is born outside Britain. It is likely that a new Nationality Act will be passed by the British Government that will change this, but until then a British mother married to a Spaniard can give her child British nationality only by returning to Britain for the birth.

American law is different. A child born in Spain of an

American father is an American citizen by birth; so also is the child of an American mother married to a Spaniard, provided that she has lived in America for at least five years before her fourteenth birthday.

Not only does Spanish law state that a child born in Spain of a Spanish father has Spanish nationality, but this is also the case when the father is a foreigner who was himself born in Spain. However, such a father, if British, has the right to give his child British nationality by registering the birth at a British consulate within one year.

In these two cases the child has dual nationality from birth. Under Spanish law such a child must, between the ages of eighteen and nineteen make a formal declaration as to whether he wishes to be a Spanish National or retain his American nationality through his mother in the first case, or his British nationality through his father in the second case. He cannot continue to have dual nationality.

Marriage does not of itself change the nationality of either partner, though it usually gives the right to change nationality. For example, under Section 6 (2) of the British Nationality Act of 1948, a Spanish girl who marries a British subject has the right to apply for British nationality, but if this is granted, she forfeits her right to Spanish nationality.

A British girl who marries a Spanish subject also has the right to apply for Spanish nationality, even if she has never previously lived in Spain. A British man who marries a Spanish girl has also the right to become a Spanish national, but only if he has lived in Spain for at least two years before the marriage. American citizens have the same rights.

Apart from marriage, any foreigner who has lived in Spain continuously for ten years can apply to become a Spanish national. The reasons for taking this step vary from person to person, but the effect of becoming a Spanish national will be to give him or her all the rights and obligations of a natural-born Spanish subject, including the right to work and live permanently in Spain without the need for a work permit or a residence permit.

CHAPTER 14

Wine

When I first came to live in Spain, I soon discovered one blessing that I had not expected, and that was the quality and cheapness of Spanish wine. I was, of course, looking forward to drinking sherry, but on my numerous holidays in Spain over very many years I had not been impressed by the table-wines.

We emigrated to Spain in 1971 and, travelling by the Southampton–Bilbao ferry, set foot on Spanish soil on 1st October. If I remember rightly, it was the very next day that we had our first pleasant surprise. Between Merida and Seville we stopped at a small modest restaurant for lunch and had a bottle of cheap red wine. It was delightful and far better than the usual French *vin ordinaire*. One peculiar feature was that it had a gold label. A few months later I discovered it again. It was a simple Valdepeñas matured in La Linea, within sight of Gibraltar, and bottled in its third year. There is also a white version with a silver label.

It was not long before we decided to make it our daily wine. Of course, today it is more expensive: now it is 41 pesetas a bottle; but where else in the world does a bottle of pleasant wine cost only 29 pence? This wine is obtainable all over the Costa del Sol, and at most restaurants should cost between 70 pence and £1. Called "Mesonero", it is only one of many other good everyday wines too numerous to mention. These "*corriente*" wines are often served in jars.

A few years later I decided to find out more about Spanish

wine and for many months visited *bodegas* all over the country. In this chapter I will describe some of the interesting things I discovered, because if you live – or work – in Spain, you must enjoy its wines, and the more you learn, the more you come to appreciate them.

Did you know that Spain has more vines under cultivation than any other European country? And that wine has been made here for more than two thousand years? It certainly came as a surprise to me. The Romans, in fact, first discovered that Spain had the ideal climate for cultivating the vine, and under their rule were developed many wine districts we know today, such as Valdepeñas, Barcelona, Tarragona and, of course, the sherry area, then known as "Betica". The famous Rioja district was developed much later.

In those far off days great quantities of wine were shipped to Imperial Rome. Behind the British Cemetary in Rome today one can see a great mound called "Monte Testacio": it is composed entirely of broken amphorae that were used to transport Spanish wine, oil and grain up the River Tiber.

With such a wonderful climate, and two thousand years' experience of making wine, Spain could be the leading wine country in the world, but it is France, Germany and Italy that have the reputation for making the best table-wines, and Spanish table-wines are dismissed by the connoisseurs as "plonk" – not to be taken seriously.

The principal reason for this paradox is that so much wine has been produced in Spain for so long that, until very recently, the Spaniards themselves did not take it seriously. A supreme example of familiarity breeding contempt. They found it too easy to make vast quantities of inferior wine quickly and cheaply and sell it in bulk to other European countries to strengthen their local wines.

France lacks the reliable sunshine of Spain, and in consequence some of the French wines do not contain enough natural sugars and need to be blended with stronger wine to achieve a proper balance. Even Chaucer in the fourteenth century said that it was common practice for French wine to be blended with Spanish – and he should have known, for his father was a vintner.

Only fifty years ago cheap wine from Tarragona was on sale in England. Called "Red Biddy" or "Poor Man's Port", rough and with an alcoholic content as high as thirty per cent, it did great harm to the reputation of Spanish wines – and little good to those who drank it. It is only fair to state that Tarragona has now redeemed itself and makes some excellent red dessert-wines, the "*Vinos Generosos*". A particularly good example is a sweet red Priorato wine with the name "Spanish Gold" produced by the old family firm of Amigó at Reus. Unfortunately port is usually unobtainable in Spain, but present-day Tarragona wines are well worth trying as a substitute.

Apart from sherry and Málaga sweet wine, it was not until late in the nineteenth century that Spain began to make wines of quality. The pioneers were the Marqués de Murrieta and Marqués de Riscal in the Rioja, Amigó in Tarragona and Miguel Torres in Vilafranca del Penédes, near Barcelona. Also, when the French vineyards were ravaged by the phylloxera beetle between 1850 and 1860, two Frenchmen came to Spain and started the well-known *bodegas* of Franco-Españoles and René Barbier.

Many years had to pass before these good wines were exported in any quantity and their quality appreciated. Indeed, even today I do not think that the best Spanish table-wines receive their due credit, either in Britain or in Spain.

Two important factors that determine the style and quality of any wine are the climate and soil, and this is well illustrated in a large country such as Spain. It can be divided into three approximately equal parts. By drawing a line on the map between Vigo near the Portuguese frontier in the north-west to just south of Tarragona in the east, and another line from Merida in the west to Alicante on the Mediterranean coast, one has three zones, each of which produces its own characteristic wines.

It is from the northern zone that the top table-wines come. It has hot summers, cold winters and plenty of rain at the right time. Here one finds the wines of the Rioja, Penédes, Tarragona, Cariñena and Ribiero. The latter are delicious dry white wines but unfortunately do not travel well and are practically unknown in Britain. If you decide to make your future home in Galicia, you will grow very fond of the white Ribieros.

The central zone produces the greatest quantity of table-wines, especially from the districts of La Mancha and Valdepeñas south of Madrid. Here the climate is hotter and arid and the wine generally not of such high quality, but there are exceptions. Jumilla and Yecla wines on the Mediterranean are popular, but not everyone likes their robustness, and their alcoholic content can be as high as seventeen per cent, which is a lot for a table-wine. This central zone is principally the home of the "*corriente*" wines – honest, everyday wines which are often pleasant and remarkably cheap.

Finally we come to the southern zone, where both climate and soil are unsuitable for making good table-wines. There is not enough rain, and much of the soil is poor, but it is ideal for aperitif and dessert-wines which need grapes with a high concentration of sugar that make a wine strong in alcohol.

In the east are produced the Málaga sweet wines, which date back to Roman times, were surreptitiously drunk by the Arabs (Mahommed was against all forms of alcohol) and became very popular in Britain in the eighteenth and nineteenth centuries. Today they are not exported in any significant quantities but are much enjoyed by those residents on the Costa del Sol who have a sweet tooth. In the hills behind the Costa del Sol, as far up as Córdoba, are made the Montilla–Moriles aperitif wines, which I can thoroughly recommend as an appetizer.

This southern zone is, however, specially famous for the production of sherry, Spain's unique and noblest of wines which is made in a very small area close to the Atlantic coast. Indeed, true sherry has by law to be matured in oak barrels in one of three towns, Jerez de la Frontera, El Puerto de Santa María and Sanlúcar de Barrameda – all within 15 miles of each other.

Sherry has had a very close association with Britain for five hundred years, though in Shakespeare's time, under its old name of "sack", it probably bore little resemblance to the sherry we know today. Modern sherry was first made at the beginning of the eighteenth century and was largely promoted by such British pioneers as Sandeman, Garvey, Osborne, Terry and Duff Gordon. A little later came Williams & Humbert who have the distinction of being the first to export a Fino to America, before the days of prohibition. This wine, Pando, is still on the market.

The two largest sherry *bodegas* are those of Domecq and González Byass. The Domecqs came from France, but the father of the Pre-Raphaelite painter and writer, John Ruskin, was once a partner, and Byass was a Welshman. The largest importers of sherry are Harveys of Bristol, who, oddly enough, until a few years ago were shippers only and never owned a single vine.

The soil in this south-west region of Spain is composed principally of chalk, with a little clay and sand, and would support no other crop than the hardy sherry vines. Their roots grow to immense depths in search of moisture, and it is said that the harder they fight for their existence, the better is the wine.

Among all other wines of the world, sherry is unique in many ways. It is made basically from one grape, the Palomino, though other grapes are used in the later stages for sweetening and colouring. Unlike other wines, it is matured in the presence of air and is always first completely fermented into a pale white dry wine. Its most distinctive features are, however, a special yeast called "*flor*" – or "*flor del vino*": the "flower of the wine", and the fact that all sherry is matured and blended in rows of oak barrels, known as a "*solera*".

The "*flor*" spontaneously appears on the surface of the

wine as soon as it is fermented and protects it from oxidization and from turning into vinegar. Only in the south of Spain does this phenomenon appear. It adds its own special flavour to sherry. In order to appreciate it, half-fill a glass with a dry Fino and then, holding it by the stem, swirl it gently round under your nose.

The other feature peculiar to sherry is its blending and ageing in the *solera*. Anyone who has visited the vast sherry *bodegas* – so aptly called "cathedrals of wine" – will have noticed the rows and rows of barrels reaching high overhead. These form the *solera*. The young fermented wine from each harvest is poured into the top row, already partly filled with wine of the same type from previous harvests. The second and subsequent rows are full of even older wine, down to the bottom row which contains the fully-matured and blended sherry. It is from this bottom row that the wine is drawn off and bottled and replaced by wine from the row above.

Each row of barrels is called a "scale", and it takes many years for the wine from a particular harvest to reach the bottom scale. The number of scales may be three, five or even more. I have come across one sherry *solera* which had as many as fifteen scales. As it is usual to draw off only about a third of a barrel each year, the wine from a *solera* with fifteen scales will have been matured for nearly fifty years. Sometimes, after the *solera*, sherry spends even more time resting and ageing in barrel. Williams & Humbert have a very special sherry which has spent ninety years in barrel. It must surely be the oldest drinkable wine in the world. They call it "a wine fit for kings".

There are many different types of sherry to suit all tastes and every occasion, from the light dry Finos to the heavy Cream Olorosos. In the Finos the *flor* is allowed to remain throughout the maturing in the *solera*, whereas in the Olorosos grape alcohol is added at an early stage which kills the *flor*. Sometimes a sherry is a blend of a Fino and an Oloroso. Williams & Humbert's Dry Sack is the best known example.

Apart from the normal dry Finos, such as Tio Pepe and La Ina, there are other Fino types, called Amontillados and Manzanillas.

If you have never tasted a Manzanilla, you should do so at the first opportunity. It is very light and dry and goes excellently with shell-fish. It has been found possible to mature a Manzanilla only at Sanlúcar de Barrameda. When matured at either of the other two sherry towns, it always turns into a normal Fino, so it seems that the Atlantic breezes of Sanlúcar are essential to this "wine of the sea".

There are even more types of Olorosos. They can be completely dry, medium sweet, very sweet, pale or nutty brown, and there is a very special old dry Oloroso called a "Palo Cortado".

It would take a whole book to describe the fascinating and complicated process of making sherry. If you are interested in learning more I suggest you read *Sherry – The Noble Wine* by Sir Manuel M. González Gordon, KBE. He is one of the happiest men that I have ever met, and his Spanish title is, most appropriately, the Marqués de Bonanza.

Of one thing you can be certain. A sherry from any of the very many *bodegas* in the three sherry towns will always be a good sherry, and its style will always be the same, year after year – the *solera* system of blending sees to that.

The Montilla-Moriles wines in this southern zone are made in almost the same way as sherry and have the same variety of types. The two differences are that they are usually fermented in large open "Ali Baba" jars, and the basic grape is the Pedro Ximénez. This grape is also used to sweeten the cream Olorosos of Jerez. It gives a special golden colour to Montilla wines.

Sherry has for centuries been accepted as the great wine of Spain, but the quality of the table-wines is only just beginning to be recognized.

The Rioja wines are today acknowledged to be the best, and this is due to the pioneers, such as the Marqués de Riscal and the Marqués de Murrietta, and to the large firms of Bilbainas and CUNE (La Compañia Vinícola del Norte de España). These four *bodegas* were winning medals at international wine festivals at the turn of the Century, but not all Rioja wines were as good as theirs.

More was needed than a few exceptional *bodegas*. Wine laws were essential to raise the standard of Spanish wines. The French have had wine laws for over a hundred years, and the certificate of "*Appellation Controlée*" guarantees the quality and origin of their best wines, that of "*Vins Delimités de Qualité Supérieure*" their cheaper wines, and "*Vins du Pays*" their everyday wines.

Spain's first wine laws were not introduced until the 1920s. They introduced the certificate of "*Denominación de Origen*" as a guarantee that a wine had been properly made with the right grapes from healthy vines, carefully fermented at the right temperature and then matured correctly. On 26th October 1926 the Rioja became the first "denominated" region, and in 1928 a controlling Council was set up, the *Consejo Regulador de la Denominación de Origen "Rioja"*. Ever since then all Rioja wines that have been properly made and matured in oak for at least two years have borne the official stamp of the *Consejo Regulador*. If you are offered a Rioja wine that you do not know, look for a small pink stamp with the name "Rioja" printed diagonally across it. It is your guarantee that the wine has been made strictly according to the regulations.

It takes time for new laws to become really effective and proper controls to be set up, and even longer before the improvement in wines becomes universally recognized. Today Spanish wine laws have become much stricter and extend to practically every wine-producing district. I remember a few years ago discussing these laws with a wine-maker in Tarragona, a very honest and dedicated man and the great-grandson of the founder of the family business. He said with a smile, "Every year it is becoming more and more difficult to cheat."

The latest statute controlling wine production was passed

in 1970, and contains 134 sections. They lay down for each region the type of vines that can be used, the method of planting, cultivation, vinification and maturing. Minimum levels of alcoholic strength for each different type of wine are prescribed and also the permissible amount of natural sugar, and finally the statute states that nothing must be added which could be harmful to health.

Naturally the standards laid down for each district vary according to the type of wine produced, from a simple and cheap Valdepeñas to an expensive Rioja. A team of inspectors are employed to see that these laws are observed, and very stiff penalties are imposed for any breach. A *bodega* that breaks the law can be fined heavily, its stock of wines confiscated, and in a bad case be closed down altogether.

The strictest regulations for table wines today are those applying to the Penedés region south of Barcelona. To qualify for the official stamp, "*Denominación Penedés*", the following conditions have to be observed.

1 Only approved types of grape can be used. Different grapes are prescribed for white and red wines.
2 Yields are limited to 55 hectolitres a hectare for red wines and 65 hectolitres for white wines.
3 The grapes cannot be harvested until the *Consejo Regulador* is satisfied that they are fully ripe and the vines are free of disease.
4 Presses of the "continuous" type are forbidden.
5 The temperature, cleanliness and sterility of the cellars are controlled.
6 Minimum standards of alcoholic strength are laid down for each type of wine.
7 White wines must be matured in oak for at least nine months, and red wines for at least eighteen months.
8 All wine must be bottled in its district of production, and the labels must show the official control number or code.

Few countries have such a large range of wines as Spain,

but the present wine laws ensure that, whether you buy a cheap, young wine or an expensive wine that has been carefully matured for years, it will be an honest wine and not harmful to health.

If anyone tells you today that Spanish wines are "doctored" or "mixed with horrid chemicals", he does not know what he is talking about. You can enjoy drinking wine in Spain without any misgivings – provided of course that the wine is from a sealed bottle.

The Rioja table-wines are made after the fashion of a Bordeaux, and in general the *bodegas* follow French methods of cultivation, fermentation and ageing, but there are some differences. Although a bare hundred miles away from the Bordeaux vineyards, the climate and soil of the Rioja are not the same, and a large variety of Spanish grapes are used. Unlike the normal practice in France, a Rioja wine is usually a blend of several vineyards, and both white and red wines spend much longer maturing in oak barrels. It is this that gives the older Riojas their characteristic oaky flavour.

In Spain one can usually rely on plenty of sun to ripen the grapes, and therefore there is no need to separate the good years from the bad ones. A few *bodegas*, such as Murrieta, Riscal, CUNE and Bilbainas, from time to time declare a vintage wine made from a single harvest, but the normal practice is to aim at a standard quality of wine year after year, which is often a blend of several harvests. Age is more important in a Rioja than its vintage.

It is therefore wrong to make a direct comparison between a Rioja and a Bordeaux: the Spanish wines have their own individual characteristics. Do not be misled by the word "*clarete*" on a Rioja label. It is nothing to do with the English word "claret" used for a red Bordeaux. "*Clarete*" is a Spanish word to describe a light red wine from the Rioja.

Most of the Rioja *bodegas* are much larger than the French *châteaux* and usually make at least three ranges of red wines, the pleasant and comparatively cheap two-year-old wines, the excellent five-year-old and the superb "Reserva" wines that have been matured in oak for seven, ten or even more years.

Rioja wines were the first to be "denominated" and are still the best-known Spanish table-wines of quality, but other regions in this northern zone today make excellent wines. In the Province of Tarragona I have much enjoyed the red, white and rosé wines made by Amigó Hermanos y Cia, de Muller and López Bertrán. Just north of Barcelona there is the Alella Bodega where a small quantity of young exquisite wine is made under the trade name "Marfil", which is Spanish for "ivory". Unfortunately they are usually on sale only in the north of Spain. If you find yourself with a few minutes to spare at Barcelona airport, refresh yourself with a glass or two of Marfil – tinto, blanco or rosado.

The denominated districts of Ribiero, Navarra, Valdeorras and Cariñena also produce table-wines, and in Vallodolid is made one of the rarest and most beautiful wines, Vega Sicilia. It is probably the best – and certainly the most expensive – table-wine in the whole of Spain. It could be described as the Spanish Romanée–Conti and is reminiscent of that world-famous Burgundy. I first discovered it in a Belgian restaurant on the Costa del Sol. A cheaper and younger version (three and five years old) is called Valbuena. Both are extremely difficult to find.

It is, however, in the denominated region of Penedés, which stretches from the holiday resort of Sitges to high up in the mountains, that one finds wines which are beginning to rival those of the Rioja. They are made from a large variety of grapes which are harvested over several weeks as the vineyards lie at different heights above sea-level. Unlike those from the Rioja, the Penedés wines spend less time maturing in barrel and much longer ageing in bottle. This gives the red wines a flavour nearer to a French Burgundy.

Reliable *bodegas* in this region are Segura Viudas, which makes both the Conde de Caralt and René Barbier wines, Freixedas, Francisco Olivella and Robert Malvasia. The largest is, however, that of Miguel Torres, situated in the picturesque town of Vilafranca del Penedés. The Torres family, from father to son, have been making good wine for centuries and started exporting over a hundred years ago. Their wines are now drunk in over seventy countries, including France. The present managing director is Miguel Torres junior, who graduated as a French oenologist at Dijon University. Of all the many Spanish viniculturists I have met, none has been more dedicated to making good wine and the constant search for perfection than Miguel Torres. In the last twenty years he has been making experiments with a variety of French grapes, such as the famous Cabernet Sauvignon. Today he sells a semi-dry white wine made from old Alsatian vines, called Viña Esmeralda, and also a superb red wine, Viña Santa Digna, made from the Pinot Noir grape from Burgundy. Other Torres wines are the dry white Viña Sol, the sweet white San Valentin, the dry rosé Rosado de Casta, and the two reds called Tres Torres (in Spain Sangre de Toro) and Coronas. These red wines and Viña Sol are also produced as Gran Reservas, which are true vintage wines from selected harvests.

You do not have to wait till you emigrate to Spain to savour Torres wines, as all those I have mentioned can be bought from many British wine-merchants for far less than comparable French wines.

In this region of Penedés one also finds the best Spanish sparkling wines made in the slow and complicated process of secondary fermentation in bottle, the "*méthode champenoise*". I wish I could call them Spanish Champagne, but unfortunately since 1960 a decision of the British High Court restricts the use of the name "Champagne" to the French wines made in the Champagne district between Rheims and Epernay. Seven years later the same court decided that, although true sherry was made only in Spain, other aperitif wines could continue to be sold under such names as "Cyprus Sherry" and "South African Sherry" because they had been sold on world markets for many years. It is a pity that the judge in the Champagne Case did not give more consideration to the fact that sparkling wine had been made in Spain in exactly the same manner as French Champagne since 1872. The correct name for such Spanish wine is now "Cava".

There are other, inferior ways of making sparkling wine, both in France and Spain. There is the "*cuve close*" method of carrying out the secondary fermentation in a tank instead of in bottle, and also the cheap and horrid method of pumping carbon dioxide gas into a still white wine. When buying Spanish sparkling wine, look for the name Cava on the label. It is your guarantee that it has been made correctly by the "*méthode champenoise*".

The little hill town of San Sadurní de Noya in the Penedés district is given over entirely to the production of Spanish Cava wine. Here one finds such famous producers as Codorníu, Freixenet and Castellblanch, to name only a few. Codorniú is the oldest and has vast caves for maturing the wine, far exceeding any found in France. It is not usual for these firms to make normal non-sparkling table-wines, but there are two outstanding exceptions. Just outside San Sadurní de Noya are the *bodegas* of Segura Viudas, who make Cava wines, under their own name and also under the name Conde de Caralt. These wines are in addition to their Conde de Caralt and René Barbier table-wines. The largest Rioja *bodega* of Bilbainas also makes an excellent Cava wine called Royal Carlton.

Spanish Cava at its best is excellent but has a different flavour from French champagne, because Spanish grapes are used and the climate and soil of the Penedés district is not the same as that of northern France. The Spanish also tend to make their sparkling wines much sweeter than the French. Even if the label says "*Seco*", it will not be really dry. It is necessary to find one labelled "*Brut*" or "*Bruto*".

A chapter on Spanish wine would not be complete without a mention of the many Spanish brandies, because they are truly the spirit of wine. The name "brandy" is derived from the Dutch word "*brandewijn*" which means "burnt wine".

This is an apt description of how it is made, because wine is first heated in a container, an alembic, until the alcohol vaporizes. It is then cooled in a condenser and liquefies into a raw spirit. This spirit after maturing in oak barrels becomes brandy.

The cheap and quick way of making brandy is in a large "continuous" still, but the best Spanish brandies are made in a discontinuous process carried out in two stages by the "*méthode chavantais*" as in France. This removes all the unwanted elements in the heated wine.

In Andalusia the Spanish make their own particular style of brandy. The spirit is first matured in oak casks, which have previously contained sherry, usually an old Amontillado or Oloroso, which gives it a distinctive flavour. Then it is blended like sherry in a *solera*. The barrels are placed in long rows on top of each other. As the fully-aged brandy is drawn off the bottom barrels, what remains is mixed with younger spirit from other barrels above. In this way not only is the brandy continually revitalized but the quality is kept constant.

Practically all the sherry *bodegas* make several styles of brandy, often using wine bought in bulk from other parts of Spain, such as Valdepeñas and La Mancha. The cheapest are sometimes rough but warming, but the top *solera* brandies can be excellent. They are, however, unlike a good French cognac, being sweeter and more caramelized. A dash of cheap *solera* brandy greatly improves a cup of coffee.

Many of the well-known producers of wine in north-east Spain also make good brandy from the second or third pressings of the grapes, which are not suitable for table-wine. The careful distillation and maturing of the spirit are more important in a brandy than the quality of the original wine. However, the Torres *Bodegas* in Vilafranca del Penedés have for a long time specialized in making the best possible brandy from grapes grown in their own vineyards which have been cultivated for this sole purpose. They have supplied Barcelona with brandy for well over fifty years. In Spain they sell a five-year-old, and three much older styles, called Grand Rouge, Fontenac and Hors d'Age. On the British market at the present time there are three ranges under the names Miguel III, Miguel II and Ministro "Black Label". These Torres brandies are not cheap, but the price of a French brandy in Spain is astronomical.

Finally, there are many wine-based liqueurs made in Spain under licence, such as Cointreau at Vilafranca del Penedés, Pernod at Tarragona, Benedictine in Madrid and Marie Brizard in the Basque country. The most interesting of these is Chartreuse which can claim to be truly Spanish as well as French.

The basis of all Chartreuse is a secret formula which came into the hands of the Carthusian monks at the beginning of the seventeenth century. For years the monks made both Green and Yellow Chartreuse at their head monastery at La Grande Chartreuse in the mountains near Grenoble. Then in 1903 they were banished from France and fled to Spain. At Tarragona they built a distillery near the port, which has been the home of Spanish Chartreuse ever since. It was not until 1940 that the monks were allowed to return to France, so for thirty-seven years all Chartreuse was made in Spain.

The original secret formula is now kept under lock and key at La Grande Chartreuse, and only three monks, between them, know the complicated process of mixing the rare herbs with the wine spirit in exactly the right proportions. Green Chartreuse has no fewer than 130 different herbs. Today the monks work from January to May in Spain and return to France for the rest of the year.

Green Chartreuse is the purest of all liqueurs. Nothing is added to the wine spirit and herbs except water, sugar and small amounts of honey. The brilliant clear colours of both types come solely from the herbs. The green is produced by the natural chlorophyll in the herbs, and the yellow comes from the autumn crocus saffron. To preserve this clarity the liqueur is aged in small barrels of white Russian oak.

Chartreuse has been called "the king of liqueurs" and "the

elixir of long life". To appreciate its quality, it must be savoured in small sips, because it is the strongest of all liqueurs, and much stronger than any brandy. Green Chartreuse is more than half pure alcohol – in fact no less than 96.36 per cent proof.

Alphonse Daudet in *Lettres de mon Moulin* has described the effect of drinking Green Chartreuse with the memorable words – "*J'en eu l'estomac tout ensoleillé*".

CHAPTER 16

Enjoying Spain

The Spaniards have a traditional toast: '*Salud, Pesetas – y Amor*', 'Health, Prosperity – and Love'.

Money is, of course, a most important consideration when planning your life in Spain, but there are other things that matter even more. Health, love and keeping active are essential for a full and enjoyable life. All the money in the world will not make up for boredom. However carefully you have planned your future in Spain, it will not be a success without these three basic human requirements.

I cannot help you in matters of health, and I would not dare to discuss your love life. I hope you come to Spain with your body and heart intact. Indeed, the sun and wine will be good for your health and, who knows, if you are looking for love, it may be waiting for you on these fabled shores. The one thing left is how to use your new-found leisure.

Luckily there is really no reason why this should cause a problem, because Spain offers so much in leisure-time activities.

The first thing you will discover is the very full social life that exists among the English-speaking communities. I think this is because they all have one factor in common: they have all taken the plunge and started a fresh life in a new and exciting country. Later you will make friends with the Spaniards and come to appreciate their outlook on life. They are a happy, warm-hearted people and will soon make you welcome. They love their country and are flattered that you have chosen it as your home.

My first experience of this was when we had finished a long and rather tedious annual general meeting of our local Association of Owners. It was late, and many of us went to a nearby restaurant. After the meal we adjourned to a private room upstairs. Out came the guitars, and we all danced the *Sevillana* until dawn. My wife and I were the only British people present and felt proud to be the guests of our Spanish neighbours as they 'let their hair down' and enjoyed themselves with typical Andalusian enthusiasm. They have a real zest for life.

I also remember 'seeing the New Year in' with a Spanish family. First we inspected the children's model crib, where each day the Wise Men with their gifts are advanced one inch towards the cradle until they finally reach it on 6th January, the Spanish 'Festival of the Three Kings'. Then we adjourned to the sitting-room for a buffet supper where wine and conversation flowed. It is amazing how a little alcohol improves one's Spanish. Finally came midnight, and the television was turned on.

As the twelve strokes of the clock rang out, we each ate our twelve grapes in the age-long tradition and drank a toast to future happiness in the coming twelve months. Finally we said good-bye – the warm hand-shakes, the women's cheeks to be kissed. Once again we had experienced the typical Spanish hospitality, symbolized by the greeting you hear all over Spain, '*Mi casa es su casa*' – 'My house is your house'.

New friends, British, Spanish and many other nationalities, will play an important part in your life. But more is needed for full enjoyment, and luckily Spain offers a wide choice of activities and hobbies to suit everyone.

For some this will be a chance to catch up with reading. Many English books are for sale or can be borrowed from libraries, and most English newspapers are available, often the day after they are published. In an appendix I list some newspapers and magazines in English that are published in Spain. And you never know, one day you may find yourself reading Spanish.

A great number of British and American clubs and societies provide a large range of social activities from amateur dramatics to bridge-parties and film shows. The Spanish themselves offer you flamenco, *fiestas*, bull-fights, football, night-clubs, concerts and international ballet, and recently casinos have been legalized where you can try your luck at roulette, *chemin-de-fer* and *baccarat*. The great variety and beauty of the countryside is a constant temptation to the photographer and painter. Spanish architecture is justly world-famous, and the museums and art collections are full of priceless treasures. Visits can be made to little *pueblos* on the *sierras* where time stands still. Indeed, it is difficult to think of any hobby or interest that cannot be enjoyed in Spain, from polo, swimming and dog-breeding to bird-watching and winter sports.

The wonderful climate makes it possible to pursue outdoor sports all the year round wherever you live, in the north or the south, in the mountains or on the coast. The gardener, the golfer, the hunter, the fisherman and the sailing enthusiast will be very happy. Let us consider some of these activities in more detail.

GARDENING

Almost any flower or shrub that grows in England will grow in Spain, but it will be in bloom for much longer and often be two or three times the size. You can pick roses most of the year and indeed will often have to sacrifice the flowers when it comes to pruning. Emigration does not mean saying good-bye to your favourite flowers: irises, marguerites, arum lilies, geraniums, violets, petunias and many others will flower early and abundantly under the Spanish sun – always provided that they have enough water.

In addition there are varieties that do not flourish in England, such as bougainvillea, hibiscus and mimosa, and many ornamental shrubs and trees. The local nurseries, called '*viveros*', will advise which are best for a particular situation. For the first time in your life your garden can produce pomegranates, lemons, oranges and tangerines. I have found it most satisfying to eat marmalade made from my own oranges, particularly when flavoured with a little local gin.

Flat-dwellers can cultivate the Spanish art of 'gardening in pots', masses of pots of all shapes and sizes. They cluster round doors and on balconies, or, even better, hang on hooks so that glowing colours cascade down white walls.

A keen gardener will find much enjoyment, and 'green fingers' will seldom be still.

GOLF

Golf has become a very popular sport in Spain among all nationalities, and today there are some fifty courses throughout the country. They have been planned in areas of great natural beauty and are of such excellent quality that they are in great demand for international events both amateur and professional. Some of the best known are the Real Sociedad Hipica Español Club de Campo in Madrid, the Real Sociedad de Golf de Neguri in Viscaya, the Real Club de Golf el Prat, Barcelona, the Club de Golf Terramar in Sitges and El Saler, Parador Luis Vives, near Valencia, while on the Costa del Sol there are many more, such as Sotogrande, Nueva Andalucía, Golf Guadalmina, Los Monteros and Club Atalaya Park.

Many of these golf-courses provide additional facilities such as riding, tennis, polo, swimming and even hockey and clay-pigeon shooting. I was talking the other day to a keen golfer – he is a member of the Royal and Ancient – and he had nothing but praise for Spanish courses. The normal green fees are 600 pesetas a day.

YACHTING

Spain has no less than 4,000 miles of coastline and about a hundred large lakes, and so, not surprisingly, it is a yachtsman's paradise. The Atlantic coast has more than a hundred good harbours, and the Mediterranean nearly as many.

Every year more yachting harbours are being built, and often they are combined with a development of flats, shops and restaurants. The Puerto José Banus near Marbella is a typical example.

For further information the following names and addresses will be useful:

Ministerio de Marina, Montalbán 2, Madrid.

Federación Español de Vela, Juan Vigón, Madrid.

Federación Español de Motonáutica, Avenida de America 33, Madrid.

WINTER SPORTS

At first sight one would not associate sunny Spain with winter sports, but it is a country with some of the highest mountains in Europe, and skiing is possible from November right up till May, and sometimes even June.

Naturally most resorts are found in the north, in the Pyrenees and the mountains of Galicia, but there are several around Madrid in the Guadarrama and Gredos Sierras, and also the Sierra de Gudar near Teruel. Except for the Costa Brava, where several resorts exist in the Provinces of Barcelona, Gerona and Lerida, winter sports are not found near the eastern Mediterranean coast.

On the Costa del Sol, however, the Sierra Nevada near Granada provides some of the best skiing in Spain; indeed, it is claimed by the locals to be the finest in Europe. With a snow area of 24 square miles, it is an easy three hours' drive from Málaga. You can stay in a National Parador, the four-star Hotel Melia or several cheaper places. Flats are also available to buy or to let. There are nursery slopes and slopes only suitable for experts. In fact one run is 7 kilometres long and involves a descent of more than 4,000 feet. The ski school at Solynieve has fifty qualified instructors, and the charges run from 800 pesetas an hour for individual tuition, to only 280 pesetas for two hours in large groups. Further information can be obtained from Federación Andaluza de

Esqui, Paseo de Ronda 78, Granada.

HUNTING GAME

Ten main species of big game exist in Spain today: deer, stag, ibex, roebuck, mountain goat, boar, wolf, lynx, bear and mountain sheep. Of these only the lynx is completely protected, and special limitations apply to bears. The best areas are the Atlantic coast; the Pyrenees; between Toledo and Córdoba; and in the south a large area north of Seville and also between Granada and Málaga. Hunting starts in the middle of September and continues till the middle of February. In the Ronda National Reserve you can stalk the famous Spanish goat, *cabra hispanica*, from 15th March to 30th April, and 15th November to 31st December.

Small game can generally be hunted throughout the year and consists of partridge, water fowl, dove, capercaillie, quail, bustard, grouse, rabbit, hare and pheasant.

There are many different methods of shooting small game, from the lone gun with his dog, called '*al salto*' to the carefully prepared beat, involving many guns and beaters, called '*el ojeo*'. The latter is the method used for the famous Spanish red partridge. The area is divided into five or six plots with twelve to fourteen blinds to each plot.

The bustard offers interesting sport. It is the largest of all European birds and is not found in any great numbers outside Spain. The best areas are Andalusia and Extremadura. For a very swift-running bird, it has a most inappropriate name. It is derived from the Latin words '*avis*' and '*tarde*', which mean 'the slow bird'.

Remember that you will need a licence to hunt in Spain, also an import licence for fire-arms and special insurance. For further information write to Mr Sidney W. Malkin, Zurbano 57, Madrid.

Those who have enjoyed beagling in England can continue the sport in Spain. But instead of standing on a cold hillside watching the beagles run one way and the hare another, you will probably find yourself on horseback galloping over a *sierra* in the wake of a swift pack of greyhounds.

FISHING

If someone set out to design the ideal country for fishing, he would probably end up by inventing the Iberian peninsula. Spain is truly a fisherman's paradise.

It has a coastline which is almost equally divided between the Mediterranean and the Atlantic, and a climate varying from temperate to sub-tropical. Then there are the rivers and streams, an incredible 48,000 miles, and countless lakes and reservoirs. The variety of fish is immense, from salmon, trout, pike, mullet and carp in the rivers and lakes to mackerel, bass, swordfish and tuna – even sharks – in the sea. Whatever your favourite fish, you will find it in Spain, and many more you have never seen.

Fishing by boat goes on throughout the year, though in the north along the Cantabrian coast July and September are best for bream, whiting, bogue and conger-eels. In the Mediterranean the summer months, from May to September, are the most rewarding for swordfish, tuna and the ever-popular grouper, and trolling for mackerel and cod. If you can afford it, deep-sea fishing with special boats and equipment can reward you with catches weighing as much as 650 pounds or more.

For fresh-water fishing the best rivers flowing into the Atlantic are the Douro, Tajo, Guadiana and Guadalquivir, and those into the Mediterranean are the Ebro, Júcar and Segura – particularly in their upper reaches. For salmon the Atlantic coast from the French to the Portuguese frontiers is most popular. Here trout are found in abundance, and also in the mountain rivers and streams further inland, particularly in the large central area from west of Salamanca to the east of Teruel. Even as far south as Andalusia trout are available. At El Bosque, midway between Ronda and Arcos de la Frontera, there is a Parador which claims to be the most southerly trout hotel in Europe. It is aptly called 'the Parador Las Truchas' – I have also discovered it has an excellent wine cellar.

Information as to fishing regulations can be obtained from the provincial offices of ICONA (the National Institute for the Conservation of Nature), but this will not concern the amateur angler, provided he avoids private preserves and remembers that fishing in the sea is prohibited from one hour after sunset until one hour before dawn.

The open seasons for fresh-water fishing are as follows:

Salmon from the first Sunday in March until 18th July.

Trout from the first Sunday in March until 15th August.

High mountain river trout from 16th May to 30th September.

Sturgeon from 1st January to 31st July.

Shad from 1st January to 31st May.

River Crab on Thursdays, Saturdays and public holidays from 21st June to 31st August; the legal limit is eighty crabs a day.

Other fresh-water fish can be caught all the year round. These include mullet, sea-lamprey, barbel, bogue, tench, pickerel and black bass.

In Spain there is plenty of time. Time to do some of those things you have always wanted to do, and many others that you had never dreamed of. There is no need to worry about having nothing to do. Anyone who is bored in Spain would be bored in any country.

As a recipe for an enjoyable life, the advice once given to me by a north-country journalist cannot be bettered. He said, "Get out – Go to places – Meet people – Do things." He had the right idea.

Appendix

APPENDIX I

The New Spanish Constitution

A summary of Articles 10 to 55 which set out the fundamental rights and obligations of all citizens of Spain, including British and other foreign residents.

THE FIRST TITLE

FUNDAMENTAL RIGHTS AND OBLIGATIONS

10 *The Rights of the Individual.* The dignity of the person and consequent inviolable rights, the free development of personality, respect for the law and the rights of others are declared to be fundamental for the maintenance of political order and a peaceful society. These rights and freedoms will be protected by the law in conformity with the Universal Declaration of Human Rights and such other Treaties and International Agreements as may be ratified by Spain.

1 SPANISH NATIONALS AND FOREIGNERS

11 *Nationality.* The acquisition, maintenance and loss of Spanish nationality will be according to the existing law, but no person born with Spanish nationality can be deprived of it. In certain cases double nationality will be recognized (the Spanish-American countries and those having a particular close association with Spain).

12 *The Age of Majority.* All Spaniards become of age at eighteen.

13 *The Rights of Foreigners.* With the exception of those rights recognized in Article 23 (voting at General Elections and holding public office), all foreigners will enjoy the public rights guaranteed by this Title within the limits laid down in treaties and by the law. However, they may be allowed to vote at municipal elections where reciprocity exists between Spain and their native country. This will depend on future laws and

treaties. Extradition will depend on international treaties, but no one will be expelled for a political offence that does not amount to an act of terrorism. Laws will be passed dealing with rights of asylum of foreign nationals and stateless persons.

2 RIGHTS AND FREEDOMS

14 *Equality before the law.* All Spaniards are equal before the law without distinction of birth, race, sex, their opinions or any other personal or social circumstances.

SECTION A FUNDAMENTAL RIGHTS AND PUBLIC FREEDOMS

15 *The Right to Live.* No one shall be tortured, chastised or submitted to inhuman or degrading treatment. The death penalty will be abolished, except under military law in time of war.

16 *Religious, Ideological and Cultural Freedoms.* These freedoms are guaranteed to individuals and communities and will be limited only so far as may be necessary to preserve public order. Nobody will be obliged to declare his ideology, religion or beliefs. The State will respect the secrecy of the confessional and continue to co-operate with the Catholic Church and other religious Faiths.

17 *Personal Freedom.* No one can be deprived of his liberty, except as mentioned in this Article, and in the circumstances and in the manner laid down by law. Preventive detention shall last only for so long as may be strictly necessary for elucidating the facts of a case, and in all cases a person must be released or brought before a court within seventy-two hours. Anyone kept in custody must be informed immediately – and in a manner he can understand – of his rights and the reason for his detention. He is not obliged to make any statement and is entitled to the assistance of a lawyer in judicial and police enquiries. The law will accept the principle of "Habeas Corpus", and the maximum period of any provisional imprisonment will be determined by law.

18 *Right to Privacy.* A man is entitled as of right to privacy for himself and his family and to his good name. Without his consent his home can be entered or searched only under a judicial warrant or when a serious crime has been committed. The secrecy of all communications (especially by post, telephone and telegraph) are guaranteed, except where a court may order otherwise, and in such a case the use of any information obtained will be limited so as to protect a person's honour, his

privacy and the exercise of his rights.

19 *Freedom of Residence and Movement.* All Spaniards have the right to choose where they shall live and travel freely throughout Spain. They can leave and enter the country within the limits of the law, but such limits cannot be imposed on political or ideological grounds.

20 *Free Speech.* The free expression of thoughts, ideas and opinions are guaranteed whether by words, writing or any other form of communication. The law will recognize the dictates of conscience and professional secrets. These rights will not be subject to censorship. Official communications will be under parliamentary control, and political and social groups will have access to the media. Publications and recordings can be seized only under a court order.

21 *Meetings.* Peaceful and unarmed meetings can be held without previous permission. However, in the case of meetings or demonstrations in public places, prior information must be given to the Authorities, and they will be forbidden only if they constitute a real threat to public order or a danger to people or property.

22 *Associations.* People have the right to form associations, but those which have criminal aims or use criminal methods are illegal. Associations must be entered in a register for the sole purpose of public record, and they can be disbanded or have their activities suspended only by a court order. Secret societies or those of a para-military nature are forbidden.

23 *Public Affairs.* Spanish Nationals have the right to take part in public affairs, either in person or through their representatives who have been freely elected by universal suffrage, and they can hold public office. (These rights are not granted to foreign nationals, except when the law may permit them to vote in municipal elections where reciprocity exists.)

24 *Legal Protection.* All persons have the right of access to the courts, to be defended by a lawyer, to be informed of any charges made against them, and to have the protection of a public hearing without undue delay. They can bring evidence in their defence, refuse to make statements which might incriminate them, and – most important – are presumed innocent until proved guilty. The law will lay down those cases in which a person can refuse to disclose family or professional secrets.

25 *Imprisonment.* The object of depriving anyone of his freedom is to re-educate him so that he can return to society. There will be no forced labour. Those in prison will continue to enjoy

their basic rights, saving only those which are expressly limited because of the nature of their crime or the reason for their punishment. In all cases there will be the right to remunerative work and to receive Social Security benefits. The Civil Administration cannot impose penalties which might, directly or indirectly, result in depriving anyone of his freedom.

26 *Disciplinary Committees.* These are forbidden whether in the Civil Administration or in professional bodies.

27 *Education.* All have the right to free education with the aim of developing their full personality, and this includes the guarantee that children will receive religious and moral instruction in accordance with their family's convictions. Teachers, parents and students will take part in the control and management of schools and centres of instruction, which will be maintained out of public funds. Universities will have the right of self-government within the framework of the law. Education will be compulsory and free.

28 *Trade Unions.* Everyone is free to join a trade union, but cannot be forced to join. But this right will be limited or excluded in the case of the Armed Forces and other bodies who are subject to military discipline or who have special public functions. There are rights to form new trade unions, to affiliate with other associations – both national and international – and to form confederations of unions. Workers have the right to strike in defence of their particular interests, but there will be laws to guarantee the maintenance of essential services.

29 *Written Petitions.* All Spaniards have the right to make written petitions either individually or in association with others and in the form prescribed by law. Those subject to military discipline, however, can only exercise this right individually and subject to special laws.

SECTION B RIGHTS AND DUTIES OF CITIZENS

30 *Military Service.** The defence of Spain is both the right and the duty of the Spanish people. The law will lay down the extent of this duty, but the rights of conscientious objectors will be respected and protected. Anyone excused Military Service may be ordered instead to do some work of benefit to society. A Civil Service may also be set up to assist in matters of common interest. In cases of grave risk, catastrophy and public emergency these public duties can be altered.

31 *Taxation.* Everyone will contribute towards the needs of public

* Only Spanish nationals are liable for military service.

expenditure according to his means. There will be a just system of taxation based on the principles of equality and progress, but in no case will it amount to confiscation. Public expenditure will be reasonably adjusted in accordance with national resources, and the aim will be efficiency and economy.

32 *Marriage.* Men and women have equal rights to contract a marriage. The law will lay down the forms of marriage, the age and capacity of the parties, and their rights and duties as married couples. It will also specify the grounds for legal separation and the dissolution of the marriage, and deal with the consequent effects of these events.

33 *Property Rights.* The rights of owning and inheriting private property are recognized, but the exercise of such rights will be limited by the law. However, no one can be deprived of these rights except for reasons that are justified on public and social grounds, and compensation will be payable in accordance with the law.

34 *Endowments.* These are permitted provided they are in the public interest and in agreement with the law.

35 *The Right to Work.* All Spaniards have both the right and the duty to work, but they are free to choose the kind of work and are also entitled to promotion in that work. They have the right to remuneration that is adequate to the needs of themselves and their families. Discrimination on the grounds of sex is forbidden. The law will prepare a new Workers' Charter.

36 *The Professions.* Legal provisions will be made to protect the special rights of professional bodies to manage their own affairs and to use professional titles, but their associations must be run in a democratic manner.

37 *Labour Disputes.* The right of collective bargaining is recognized, and also the binding force of agreements made between workers and management. Measures may be adopted to overcome disputes provided they do not conflict with the existing laws. The law will, however, take steps to ensure the functioning of services essential to the community.

38 *Companies.* The freedom of companies to act according to the market economy is recognized, and the State will assist by economic planning and by promoting productivity that meets the needs of the general economy.

3 THE GOVERNING PRINCIPLES OF SOCIAL AND ECONOMIC POLICIES

39 *Family Protection.* Social, economic and legal provisions will

be made to help families. Children will be fully protected and will be considered equal in the eyes of the law without regard to their parenthood or the marital state of their mothers. The law will assist in establishing paternity. Parents have a duty to give every assistance to their children until they are of age, whether they are living at home or away, and to encourage their lawful activities. Children will enjoy the rights granted to them by international agreements.

40 *Redistribution of Wealth and Full Employment.* Policies of a stable economy will promote conditions that are favourable for social and economic progress and bring about a fairer distribution of wealth between both regions and individuals. There will be policies specially aimed at full employment, training and resettlement. Health and safety at work and the need for relaxation will be guaranteed by limiting the working day, granting holidays with pay and the provision of adequate leisure facilities.

41 *Social Security.* The State will continue to provide a system of Social Security for all by giving free assistance and financial aid to meet cases of need, especially those arising from unemployment.

42 *Emigrants.* The State will give especial attention to the economic and social interests of Spaniards working abroad and assist their return to their native country.

43 *Health.* Public health will be promoted and maintained by means of preventive measures, financial grants and necessary services. In this respect the law will lay down the rights and duties of all. Education in matters of health, physical recreation and sport will be provided, and there will be measures to facilitate adequate leisure activities.

44 *Culture.* The right of everyone to have access to culture will be safeguarded, and the State will encourage the sciences and scientific and technical research for the benefit of the general community.

45 *Living Conditions.* Everyone has a right to enjoy decent living standards so that they may develop their personalities to the full, and equally everyone has the duty to preserve those standards. Through the sensible use of natural resources, the State will endeavour to safeguard and improve the quality of life and maintain reasonable living conditions, and in this respect it relies on the full co-operation of all. If anyone violates these rights, the law will impose penalties and in addition order the reparation of any damage.

46 *The National Heritage.* The historical, cultural and artistic heritage of the Spanish people will be preserved, and legal action will be taken against any acts which may threaten it.

47 *Land Development.* All the Spanish people have the right to live in decent and adequate homes, and the State will create the necessary conditions to achieve this end, and appropriate laws will be passed to give effect to this right. In the interests of the community the use of land will be controlled, and speculative development will be prevented, because the increase in values resulting from development belongs to all.

48 *Youth.* Conditions will be created to enable young people to play their part, freely and effectively, in the political, social, economic and cultural life of Spain.

49 *The Incapacitated.* The State will ensure the treatment, rehabilitation and integration into society of all those who are handicapped, whether physically, mentally, or psychologically. They will receive specialized treatment to enable them to enjoy to the full the rights which this Title of the Constitution grants to all citizens.

50 *The Elderly.* During their "third age" people will be provided with a sufficient income by means of pensions, which will be adequate and increased from time to time. In addition, and irrespective of their family's responsibilities, the State will promote their well-being by means of social services which will meet their special problems of health, home, culture and leisure.

51 *Consumer Protection.* The State will guarantee the rights of consumers and users and will take effective measures to protect their safety, their health and their legitimate economic interests. They will be provided with information, have their problems considered and have their own organizations. In their interests the law will control the national economy and lay down minimum commercial standards.

52 *Trade Associations.* Associations formed to protect the financial interests of their members will be subject to the law, and must be run on democratic lines.

4 THE GUARANTEES OF FUNDAMENTAL RIGHTS AND FREEDOMS

53 *Protection of Rights and Freedoms.* Those rights and freedoms set out under Heading 2 of this Title (Articles 14 to 38) are the responsibility of the State. The exercise of such rights and freedoms will be subject only to laws which will respect their essential aims, and they will be guaranteed by the Constitutional

Tribunal. The rights and freedoms set out under Heading 1 (Articles 11 to 13) and Article 14 will be protected by the ordinary courts. Anyone can apply to the courts and will have a right of appeal to the Constitutional Tribunal. Conscientious objectors to Military Service (Article 30) will have a similar right of appeal. The principles set out under Heading 3 (Articles 39 to 52) will be subject to special laws, judicial interpretation and State decisions. These principles can be pleaded only before the ordinary courts in the exercise of their normal jurisdiction.

54 *Protection of the Public.* Appropriate laws to protect the public will be passed by the *Cortes Generales*, which is charged with defending the rights set out in this Title. The effectiveness of such laws will be watched by the Government in consultation with the *Cortes Generales.*

5 THE SUSPENSION OF RIGHTS AND FREEDOMS

55 *Emergencies and Terrorism.* If a State of Emergency is declared, the rights set out in the following Articles will be suspended: – 17, personal freedom (other than the right to be informed of criminal charges and have the assistance of a lawyer) – 18, privacy of home and communications – 19, freedom of movement – 20, freedom of speech – 21, meetings – 28, the right to strike – and 38, labour disputes. Appropriate laws will determine under the control of Parliament when certain rights set out in Articles 17 and 18 (relating to preventive detention and secrecy of communications) will be suspended in the case of particular persons being questioned in connection with the activities of armed bands or terrorists. Any unjustified use or abuse of these powers will be treated as a criminal offence and a violation of those rights and freedoms recognized by the law.

Note: The new Spanish Constitution was adopted by the Spanish Cortes on 31st October 1978, approved by the Spanish people in the Referendum held on 6th December 1978 and became law when signed by King Juan Carlos on 27th December 1978.

APPENDIX II

British Government Stocks

(on which the interest is tax-free to genuine foreign residents)

12¾% Exchequer Stock 1981
13¼% Exchequer Loan 1996
5½% Funding Stock 1982–4
5¾% Funding Loan 1987–91
6% Funding Loan 1993
6½% Funding Loan 1985–7
3% Treasury Stock 1982
5½% Treasury Stock 2008–12
6¾% Treasury Loan 1995–8
7¾% Treasury Loan 2012–15
7¾% Treasury Loan 1985–8
8% Treasury Loan 2002–6
8¼% Treasury Loan 1987–90
8½% Treasury Loan 1980–82
8½% Treasury Loan 1984–6
8¾% Treasury Loan 1997
9% Treasury Loan 1994
9% Treasury Loan 1992–6
9½% Treasury Loan 1999
9¾% Treasury Stock 1981
11½% Treasury Stock 1981
12% Treasury Loan 1983
12½% Treasury Loan 1993
12¾% Treasury Loan 1992
12¾% Treasury Loan 1995
13% Treasury Stock 1990
13¼% Treasury Loan 1997
13¾% Treasury Loan 1993
14% Treasury Stock 1982
14½% Treasury Loan 1994
15¼% Treasury Loan 1996
15½% Treasury Loan 1998
3½% War Loan
4% Victory Bonds

APPENDIX III

Spanish Inheritance Tax

This tax is payable on all real or personal property in Spain which passes on the death of the owner, whether such owner was living in Spain or not. The amount payable depends on the value of the property and the relationship of the beneficiary to the deceased.

Value of Assets in Pesetas		*Beneficiary*	
		Spouse and Issue	*Strangers in Blood*
Up to	10,000	3%	58%
10,001	25,000	4%	60%
25,001	50,000	6%	62%
50,001	100,000	7%	64%
100,001	250,000	8%	66%
250,001	500,000	9%	68%
500,001	1,000,000	10%	70%
1,000,001	3,000,000	12%	73%
3,000,001	10,000,000	13%	76%
10,000,001	25,000,000	15%	78%
25,000,001	50,000,000	17%	80%
50,000,001	100,000,000	19%	82%
Over	100,000,000	21%	84%

a) No tax is payable on inheritance by close relatives of gifts up to 10,000 and life assurance moneys up to 500,000.

b) Intermediate rates of tax are payable on assets passing to other relatives as follows: parents from 5% to 26%, parents-in-law and first degree collaterals (brothers and sisters) from 23% to 55%, second degree collaterals from 28% to 58%, third degree collaterals from 40% to 69%, and fourth degree collaterals from 42% to 72%.

c) If after deduction of this tax the value of the asset passing to a beneficiary exceeds 10,000,000 a surcharge is payable in addition. The rates vary from 7% to 10% for spouses and issue; and from 15% to 18% for strangers in blood.

APPENDIX IV

Money and Cheques

Rates of Exchange		*Sterling Equivalent*	
Ptas. to £	*100 Ptas.*	*1,000 Ptas.*	*1,000,000 Ptas.*
110	91p	£9.09	£9,091
115	87p	£8.69	£8,696
120	83p	£8.33	£8,333
125	80p	£8	£8,000
130	77p	£7.69	£7,692
135	74p	£7.40	£7,407
140	71p	£7.14	£7,143
145	69p	£6.89	£6,896
150	66p	£6.66	£6,666
155	64p	£6.45	£6,452
160	62p	£6.25	£6,250
165	61p	£6.06	£6,060

Writing Cheques

a) Amounts in figures should have a full stop to indicate millions and thousands, and a comma to indicate decimals. E.g. 1.500,50 – not 1,500.50 as in English.

b) Amounts in words should have "and" before the last numeral if the preceding numeral is less than a hundred. E.g. "One hundred forty and five" ("*Ciento cuarenta y cinco*") not "One hundred and forty-five" as in English. If however the preceding numeral is a hundred the word "and" is omitted. E.g. "One hundred two" ("*Ciento dos*") not "One hundred and two" as in English.

c) The Spanish for "pay bearer" is "*paquese al portador*".

d) To cross a Spanish cheque insert the words "*y Cia*" between the lines – thus 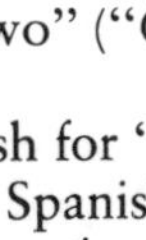 .

APPENDIX V

Telephones

Internal

Practically all Spanish telephones are now on the automatic service. When telephoning from one province to another, it is necessary first to dial the provincial code, the *Código Territorial*, as follows.

Alava	945	Ciudad Real	926
Albacete	967	Córdoba	957
Alicante	965	Coruña	981
Almeria	951	Cuenca	966
Avila	918	Gerona	972
Badajoz	924	Granada	958
Barcelona	93	Guadaljara	911
Bilbao	94	Guipuzcoa	943
Burgos	947	Huelva	955
Caceres	927	Huesca	974
Cádiz	956	Jaen	953
Castellón	964	Leon	987

Lerida	973	Santander	942
Logrono	941	Segovia	911
Lugo	982	Seville	954
Madrid	91	Soria	975
Málaga	952	Tarragona	977
Murcia	958	Toledo	925
Navarra	948	Teruel	974
Orense	988	Valencia	96
Oviedo	985	Vallodolid	983
Palencia	988	Vizcaya	94
Pontevedra	986	Zamora	988
Salamanca	923	Zaragoza	976

International

Most European countries are connected to the Spanish automatic service, except, at the moment, Gibraltar.

To telephone Britain from Spain, it is necessary to dial 07, wait until you hear a loud continuous tone, then dial 44 and continue with the full British number but omit the first digit. For example, if the number you want is 01–582377 in London you should dial 07 – (continuous tone) – 44–1–582377.

To telephone Spain from Britain one must first dial 01034, and – without waiting for any continuous tone – dial the Spanish number, but again omit the first digit of the *Código Territorial.* For example, if the number you want is 952–6074 in the province of Málaga, you should dial 01034–52–6074.

APPENDIX VI

Conversion Tables

Length

Centimetres ← inches	or cms → inches	
2·54	1	0·40
5·08	2	0·80
7·62	3	1·20
10·16	4	1·60
12·70	5	2·00
15·24	6	2·40
17·78	7	2·80
20·32	8	3·20
22·86	9	3·50
25·40	10	3·90
50·80	20	7·90
76·20	30	11·80
101·60	40	15·80
127·00	50	19·70

Kilometres ← miles	or kms → miles	
1·61	1	0·62
3·22	2	1·24
4·83	3	1·86
6·44	4	2·49
8·05	5	3·11
9·66	6	3·73
11·27	7	4·35
12·88	8	4·97
14·48	9	5·59
16·09	10	6·21
32·19	20	12·43
48·28	30	18·64
64·37	40	24·86
80·47	50	31·07

Area

Hectares ← acres or	hectares → acres	
0·41	1	2·47
0·81	2	4·94
1·21	3	7·41
1·62	4	9·88
2·02	5	12·36
2·43	6	14·83
2·83	7	17·30
3·24	8	19·77
3·64	9	22·24
4·05	10	24·71
8·09	20	49·42
12·14	30	74·13
16·19	40	98·84
20·23	50	123·60

Capacity

Litres ← gallons	or litres → gallons	
4·55	1	0·22
9·09	2	0·44
13·64	3	0·66
18·18	4	0·88
22·73	5	1·10
27·28	6	1·32
31·82	7	1·54
36·37	8	1·76
40·91	9	1·98
45·46	10	2·20
90·92	20	4·40
136·38	30	6·60
181·84	40	8·80
227·30	50	11·00

Weight

Kilogrammes ← pounds	or kgs →	pounds	Kilogrammes ← pounds	or kgs →	pounds
0·45	1	2·21	3·63	8	17·64
0·91	2	4·41	4·08	9	19·84
1·36	3	6·61	4·54	10	22·05
1·81	4	8·82	9·07	20	44·09
2·27	5	11·02	13·61	30	66·14
2·72	6	13·23	18·14	40	88·19
3·18	7	15·43	22·68	50	110·20

Temperature

°Celsius ←	°Fahrenheit
−10	14
0	32
10	50
20	68
30	86
40	104
50	122

Tyre Pressures

Lbs per sq. in.	Kgs per sq. cm.
20	1·41
22	1·55
24	1·69
26	1·83
28	1·97
30	2·11
32	2·35

Cooking Conversions

Litres	Pints	Grammes	Ounces
0·25	0·44	100	3·50
0·50	0·88	150	5·25
0·75	1·32	250	8·75
1·00	1·75	500	17·50
2·00	3·50	1,000 (1 kilo)	35·00 (2 lb 3 oz)

APPENDIX VII

Some English Schools

Madrid	British Institute School, Martinez Campos 31, Madrid-10.
	Hill House School, Avenida Alfonso X111 34/40, Madrid-2.
	Kensington School, Triana 65, Madrid.
	Kings College English School, Avenida Stuyk 1. Madrid-16.
	St Michael's Preparatory School, Agustina de Aragón 10, Madrid-6.
Barcelona	Anglo-American School, Paseo de Barbi 152,.Castelldefels, Barcelona.
	Kensington School, Carretera de Esplugas 86, Barcelona.
	St George's English School, Calle Dr Amigant 15, Sarria, Barcelona-17.
	St Paul's School, Martorell y Pena 9, Barcelona-17.
	St Peter's School, General Yague 16, Barcelona-16.
Benidorm	Lope de Vega, La Torreta-Rinson de Loix, Benidorm.
Alicante	The Sierra Bernia School, La Caneta, San Rafael, Alfaz del Pi, Alicante.
Costa del Sol	Calpe College, Apartado 200, San Pedro de Alcántara, (Málaga).
	St Anthony's International College, Fuengirola, (Málaga).
	Sunny View School, Apartado 175, Cerril del Toril, Torremolinos, (Málaga).
	The English International Academy, Carretera Cádiz 108, Torremolinos, (Málaga).
Balearics	The British School, Calle Zaragoza, Son Serra, Palma de Mallorca.
	The Ibiza International School, Apartado 438, Ibiza.
Canary Islands	The British School of Gran Canaria, El Sabinal, Tafira Alta, Gran Canaria.

APPENDIX VIII

English Language Publications

WEEKLY

The Canary Island Sun Edifício Fronton, Apartado 883, Las Palmas, Islas Canarias.

The Costa Blanca News Aptos Astoria, Calle Dr Perez Llorca, Benidorm, (Alicante).

The Iberian Daily Sun Zurbano 74, Madrid 10.

Ibiza Insight Tanic Building, San Antonio, Ibiza.

The Mallorca Daily Bulletin Calle de San Feliu, Palma de Mallorca.

MONTHLY

Costa Golf Loma de los Riscos 3, Torremolinos, (Málaga).

Guidepost Edificio España, Plaza de España, Madrid 13.

Lookout Magazine Loma de los Riscos 3, Torremolinos, (Málaga).

The Island Gazette Urbanizacion La Palmita 13, La Victoria, Tenerife, Islas Canarias.

QUARTERLY

Trade Review Camera de Comercio Britanica, Paseo de Gracia 11, Barcelona 7.

APPENDIX IX

The British Embassy and Consulates

The British Embassy, Fernando el Santo 16, Madrid – 4,
Tel. (91) 419.02.00 / 419.26.30 / 419.15.28
(The Consular Section is responsible for the Provinces of Almeria, Avila, Badajos, Caceres, Ciudad Real, Cuenca, Granada, Guadalajara, Jaen, La Coruña, Lugo, Madrid, Malaga, Orense, Pontevedra, Segovia, Soria, Salamanca, Teruel, Toledo, Valladolid, Zamora and the Territory of Melilla)

CONSULATE-GENERALS

Barcelona Consulate-General,
Avenida Generalisimo Franco 477, Barcelona – 36.
Tel. (93) 322.21.51
(Responsible for the Provinces of Barcelona, Gerona, Huesca, Lerida, Tarragona and Zaragoza)

Bilbao Consulate-General, Alameda de Urquijo 2, Bilbao – 8.
Tel. (94) 415.76.00 / 415.77.11.
(Responsible for the Provinces of Alava, Burgos, Guipuzcoa, Leon, Logroño, Navarra, Oviedo, Palencia, Santander and Vizcaya)

CONSULATES AND VICE-CONSULATES

Algeciras Consulate, Avenida Franciso Franco 11, Algeciras.
Tel. (956) 66.16.00 / 66.16.04
(Responsible for the Province of Cádiz and the Territory of Ceuta)

Alicante Consulate, Calle Canalejas 1, Alicante.
Tel. (965) 20.90.18
(Responsible for the Provinces of Albacete, Alicante, Castellon, Murcia and Valencia)

Ibiza Vice-Consulate, Avenida Bartolome Rosello 24, Ibiza.
Tel. (971) 30.18.18
(Covers the island of Ibiza)

Las Palmas Consulate, Edificio Hocas 6°, Calle Alfredo Jones 33, Puerto de la Luz, Las Palmas, Gran Canaria
Tel. (928) 26.25.08
(Responsible for the Canary Islands)

Málaga Consulate, Edificio Duquesa, Duquesa de Parcent 8, Málaga.
Tel. (952) 21.75.71 / 21.23.25
(Covers the Provinces of Almeria, Granada and Málaga)

Mallorca Consulate, Avenida Jaime 111 5, Palma de Mallorca.
Tel. (971) 21.24.45
(Responsible for the Balearic Islands)

Seville Consulate, Plaza Nueva 8, Seville.
Tel. (954) 22.88.75
(Responsible for the Provinces of Cordoba, Huelva and Seville)

Tarragona Hon. Vice-Consulate, Calle Santian 4, Tarragona.
Tel. (977) 20.12.46 / 20.52.68
(Covers the Province of Tarragona)

Tenerife Hon. Consulate, Edificio Marichal, Suarez Guerra 40, Santa Cruz de Tenerife.
Tel. (922) 24.20.00
(Covers the town of Santa Cruz de Tenerife)

Vigo Vice-Consulate, Plaza de Compostela 23, Vigo.
Tel. (986) 21.14.50 / 21.14.21
(Covers the Provinces of La Coruna, Lugo, Orense and Pontevedra)

Index

Index

Index